Student Applications Book

Great Source Education Group

a Houghton Mifflin Company

Wilmington, Massachusetts

www.greatsource.com

AUTHORS

Laura Robb
Author

Powhatan School, Boyce, Virginia
Laura Robb, author of *Reading Strategies That Work* and *Teaching Reading in Middle School,* has taught language arts at Powhatan School in Boyce, Virginia, for more than 30 years. She is a co-author of the *Reading and Writing Sourcebooks* for grades 3–5 and the *Summer Success: Reading* program. Robb also mentors and coaches teachers in Virginia public schools and speaks at conferences throughout the country on reading and writing.

Margaret Ann Richek
Contributing Author

Northeastern Illinois University, Chicago, Illinois
Margaret Ann Richek is a professor of education at Northeastern Illinois University. Her specialty is the teaching of reading. She is a former teacher in Chicago and the metropolitan Chicago area. She consults extensively for school districts. Her publications include a series of ten co-authored books, *Vocabulary for Achievement* (Grades 3-10), *The World of Words: Vocabulary for College Students*, and a co-authored text, *Reading Problems: Assessment and Teaching Strategies*. Her work is also featured in *Vocabulary Strategies That Boost Students' Reading Comprehension*.

Vicki Spandel
Contributing Author

Writing specialist Vicki Spandel was co-director of the 17-member teaching team that developed the 6-trait model for writing instruction and assessment. She is the author of more than 30 books for students and teachers, including *Daybooks of Critical Reading and Writing* (for grades 3-5) and *Write Traits Classroom Kits*. Vicki has been a language arts teacher, award-winning video producer, technical writer, journalist, freelance editor, and scoring director for numerous writing assessments. As lead trainer for Write Traits, she works as a writing consultant and visiting teacher throughout the country and develops a wide range of instructional materials for use in grades K-12.

Editorial:
Design:
Illustrations:

Developed by Nieman, Inc. with Phil LaLeike
Ronan Design: Christine Ronan, Sean O'Neill, Maria Mariottini, Victoria Mullins
Mike McConnell

Printed in the United States of America

International Standard Book Number: 0-669-49527-1
(Student Applications Book)

1 2 3 4 5 6 7 8 9—DBH—08 07 06 05 04 03 02

International Standard Book Number: 0-669-49530-1
(Student Applications Book, Teacher's Edition)

2 3 4 5 6 7 8 9—DBH—08 07 06 05 04 03

Table of Contents for Student Applications Book

Lessons

What Happens When You Read

Day in and day out, you are a reader. You read all kinds of things for all kinds of reasons. Have you ever tried to keep track of what you read? Have you ever asked yourself why you read?

What you read.

Sometimes you pick up a book and sit down for a really good read. Other times, you read without even knowing it.

Directions: Think about everything you read yesterday. Make a list here. Then compare your list with a classmate's.

List

I read these things yesterday:

the back of a cereal box	the lyrics to my favorite song
a recipe for brownies	street signs on the way to school
a sports catalog	the front page of the newspaper
school papers	directions for a video game
the first part of a novel	a note from my mom
the title of a cartoon	an email from a friend
the insert that came with my new toothbrush	the day and date on my calendar
	a price tag at the mall
the sign on my brother's door	

Why you read.

Page 23 of the *Reader's Handbook* lists six reasons to read. But why do *you* read?

Directions: Make a list of the reasons you read. (We've done the first one for you.) You can use some of the reasons in the handbook, but try to come up with a few of your own. Explain each reason.

List

Here are six reasons why I read:

1. I read for fun

   because I like to get caught up in a good book.

2. I read for school

   because I have to read at least a little in every class, including gym.

3. I read when I go to church,

   because I like to follow along in my prayer book.

4. I read to help me cook

   because I know I need to follow the recipe exactly.

5. I read to my brother

   because my Mom says I need to teach him everything I know.

6. I read while I'm at the mall

   because I need to know what's cool and how much it costs.

See yourself reading.

Reading is a process. It occurs over time—in a few minutes, in a few hours, or even in a few days if the book is very, very long or very, very good.

Directions: Draw a picture of yourself reading a really great book. Use "balloons" to show what you are thinking.

Ask questions about what you read.

What do you think about as you read? You probably ask yourself questions without even realizing it. "Listening" to your questions can help you become a better reader.

Directions: Choose a book from the classroom library that you'd like to read sometime. Write the title and author's name on the lines below. Then answer these questions about it.

Title: *Answers depend on students' book choices.*

Author's Name:

What is the book about? *Students should describe the subject or plot.*

Why are you reading? *to learn something; for fun; to find information*

What do you want to get out of your reading? *enjoyment, pleasure, information*

What kind of reading is it? *poetry, a novel, nonfiction*

Should you read slowly or quickly? *You would read a novel quickly and some types of nonfiction very slowly.*

What can you do if you don't understand something? *reread; ask for help; look up words in the dictionary*

How can you remember what you've read? *tell someone about the book; take notes*

The Reading Process

The reading process is a series of steps you take to get more from a text.

Your Reading Process

What kinds of reading habits do you have? What do you do before, during, and after reading?

Directions: Describe your own reading process. Make notes or write in full sentences.

Before Reading

I look at the cover of the book and try to guess what the book will be about and whether or not I'll like it.

During Reading

I stop every few pages and think about what I've read and whether I understand it. I take notes on important information if it's school reading. Sometimes I ask for help.

After Reading

I think about what I've read and whether I liked it. I ask about parts of the reading that aren't clear to me.

The Handbook's Reading Process

The *Reader's Handbook* has lots of suggestions about the reading process. The reading process described in your handbook is like a map. If you follow it, you can stop yourself from getting lost.

Directions: Skim pages 28–33 in the *Reader's Handbook* for the steps in the reading process. Use your own words to retell them below.

Before Reading

• Set a purpose. I'll think about why I'm reading.

• Preview. I'll look over the reading to get an idea of what it's about.

• Plan. I'll plan how to read to achieve my purpose. I'll choose the right tools.

During Reading

• Read with a purpose. I'll keep my purpose in mind so I know what to look for.

• Connect. I'll connect the reading to what I know. I'll ask questions that relate

the reading to my own life.

After Reading

• Pause and reflect. I'll think about what I've read.

• Reread. If there are parts I don't understand, I'll read them again.

• Remember. I'll remember the reading by responding or writing notes.

If you get stuck, look at the Summing Up section on page 33.

NAME ....

FOR USE WITH PAGES 36–39

Reading  Know-how

You already have plenty of reading know-how. What you need to do is figure out how to put it to use. Begin by sharpening your critical thinking skills.

Thinking Skill 1: Making Inferences

Writers don't tell you everything. Sometimes you need to figure things out on your own. An inference is something you figure out on your own, based on the evidence and your own knowledge.

Directions: Read the paragraph in the box. Then make inferences to answer the questions.

> A red-faced child with tears in her eyes sits on the sidewalk in front of a house. She is wearing a helmet. A small bike with a broken chain is lying on the grass in front of her. Next to it is an unzipped backpack. Some of the contents from the backpack are lying on the sidewalk.

Inference Chart

	Circle one.	
The child has been:	sorting through her things.	(riding her bike.)
How I know this:	She is outside, and her bike is lying next to her.	
	Circle one.	
The child has:	(fallen from the bike.)	stopped for a rest.
How I know this:	She is crying, and things are in a mess around her.	
	Circle one.	
The child feels:	(angry and upset.)	tired and bored.
How I know this:	She is red-faced, which means she is upset.	

Thinking Skill 2: Drawing Conclusions

When you draw conclusions, you look at the facts and decide what they mean. For example:

◀ **Drawing Conclusions**

Fact 1

| I see trash cans lining the street. |

Fact 2

| I smell stale garbage. |

Fact 3

| I hear the rumble of the garbage truck. |

▼

Conclusion

| Today is trash day. |

Directions: Think again about the child on the sidewalk. Write facts in the boxes. (The first one has been done for you.) Then draw a conclusion.

◀ **Drawing Conclusions**

Fact 1

| The girl is sitting on the sidewalk. |

Fact 2

| She is red-faced and teary-eyed. |

Fact 3

| Her broken bicycle is lying next to her. |

▼

Conclusion

| The girl has fallen from her bicycle and is very upset about it. |

Thinking Skill 3: Comparing and Contrasting

Comparing and contrasting means thinking about the ways in which two things are alike and different.

Directions: Put two books on your desk. Compare their size, shape, and appearance. Write your notes on this Venn Diagram.

Venn Diagram

Write notes that describe Book A here.

Write notes that describe Book B here.

Book A

Both

Book B

Title: _ _ _ _ _ _ _ _ _

Title: _ _ _ _ _ _ _ _ _

bigger

dark cover

smaller

heavier

lighter

lots of pictures

no pictures

Write what they have in common.

Thinking Skill 4: Evaluating

Evaluating is making a judgment. You say what you do and don't like about something. Deciding whether something is good or bad is also evaluating.

Directions: Look at the two books again. Then tell which book looks more interesting. Explain why.

Write a book title here.

I think   my reading book   looks more interesting because

I like the pictures, and it looks kind of fun.

Thinking Skill 5: Predicting

Predicting means guessing what will happen next based on what you know. For example, you read the first part of a book and then guess how it will end.

Directions: Think about yourself as a reader. Then make some predictions about this *Student Applications Book*.

Here's what I know about myself as a reader: I'm a fast reader, but sometimes I have trouble answering questions about what I've read. I like reading stories and novels. I don't like reading nonfiction.

I predict this book will help me learn how to improve my reading.

I think the questions will be easy /(hard) to answer. Here's why: I have trouble with questions.

I predict I (will) / will not enjoy completing the activities. Here's why: They look pretty interesting. Also, I really do want to improve my reading.

Pulling It All Together

So how can all these thinking skills help you become a better reader?

Directions: Make a list of the five important thinking skills. Tell how you think these skills can help you be a better reader. We've done the first one for you.

Thinking Skill 1: Making inferences can help me read between the lines.

Thinking Skill 2: Drawing conclusions can help me understand a reading on a deeper level.

Thinking Skill 3: Comparing and contrasting can help if I want to talk about two books or two characters in a book.

Thinking Skill 4: Evaluating is a way of telling how I feel about a reading. I can use this skill in class discussions.

Thinking Skill 5: Predicting makes reading more fun. I like to see if my prediction turns out to be true.

Reading Actively

Active readers stay involved in a text from the first page to the last. They ask themselves questions, make predictions, and hold "conversations" with the author. Practice reading actively here.

Ways of Reading Actively

Good readers mark a text as they read. They jot down their comments and make sketches. They also work to make things clear so that they understand what they are reading.

Directions: Turn to page 40 of the *Reader's Handbook.* Read the section called "Six Ways to Read Actively." Then do an active reading of this short passage from the novel *A Year Down Yonder.*

> **from *A Year Down Yonder* by Richard Peck**

1. Mark

Underline information about time and place.

It was a September morning, hazy with late summer, and now with all the years between. Mother was seeing me off at Dearborn Station in Chicago. We'd come in a taxicab because of my trunk. But Mother would ride back home on the El. There wasn't much more than a nickel in her purse, and only a sandwich for the train in mine. My ticket had pretty well cleaned us out.

2. React and Connect

Tell what you know about

the narrator.

She is young and is going on some

type of train trip. She is poor.

She is traveling by herself.

from *A Year Down Yonder* by Richard Peck, continued

3. Question

Ask a question about the narrator.

Sample: How does the narrator feel about the trip she is making?

The trunk, a small one, held every stitch of clothes I had and two or three things of Mother's that fit me. "Try not to grow too fast," she murmured. "But anyway, skirts are shorter this year."

Then we couldn't look at each other. I was fifteen, and I'd been growing like a weed. My shoes from Easter gripped my feet.

A billboard across from the station read: WASN'T <u>THE DEPRESSION</u> AWFUL?

4. Create Pictures

Make a sketch of the scene.

5. Make Things Clear

Tell about the Great Depression.

The Depression took place in the U.S. when the economy was very bad, and many people were out of work.

6. Predict

Predict where the narrator is going and why she is making the trip.

Maybe she's going to stay with a friend or relative because her mother has run out of money.

NAME ....

Reading Paragraphs

A paragraph is a number of sentences that express a single idea. Finding that idea—and figuring out what it means—is one of your most important jobs as a reader.

Step 1: Read the paragraph.

First do an active reading of the paragraph.

Directions: Read this paragraph from the nonfiction book *Volcano*. Highlight important words and phrases. Complete the sticky notes.

from *Volcano* by Patricia Lauber

Mount St. Helens was built by many eruptions over thousands of years. In each eruption hot rock from inside the earth forced its way to the surface. The rock was so hot that it was molten, or melted, and it had gases trapped in it. The name for such rock is magma. Once the molten rock reaches the surface it is called lava. In some eruptions the magma was fairly liquid. Its gases escaped gently. Lava flowed out of the volcano, cooled, and hardened. In other eruptions the magma was thick and sticky. Its gases burst out violently, carrying along sprays of molten rock. As it blasted into the sky, the rock cooled and hardened. Some of it rained down as ash—tiny bits of rock. Some rained down as pumice—frothy rock puffed up by gases.

Clarify

How did Mount St. Helens form?

It was formed by many volcanic eruptions over thousands of years.

Sketch

Draw a picture of magma erupting.

Highlight/Mark

What important words do you find?

Mount St. Helens, magma, lava, eruptions

Step 2: Find the subject.

To find the subject, ask yourself, "What is this paragraph mostly about?" You can find clues about the subject by looking at these items:

√ the title

√ the first sentence

√ names, key words, and repeated words

Directions: Answer these questions. They can help you find the subject of the paragraph from *Volcano*.

1. What is the title of the selection? Volcano

2. What is the first sentence about? The first sentence is about Mount St. Helens and how it was formed.

3. What important and repeated words did you notice? lava, eruption, hot, cooled, and hardened

4. What is the paragraph mostly about? how Mount St. Helens was formed

Step 3: Find the main idea.

The main idea is what the writer is saying about the subject. Some paragraphs have a stated main idea. In others, the main idea is implied.

Stated Main Idea Some writers come right out and tell you the main idea. When this is the case, the paragraph is said to have a stated main idea. You can usually find a stated main idea in the first or last sentence of the paragraph.

Directions: Reread the first and last sentences of the *Volcano* paragraph. Then write the main idea on the lines below.

The main idea of the paragraph is: Mount St. Helens was built by many eruptions over thousands of years.

Implied Main Idea Sometimes the author expects you to figure out the main idea on your own. To find an implied main idea, first find the subject. Then ask yourself, "What is the author saying about the subject?"

Directions: Read this paragraph from *Sarah Plain and Tall*. Underline key words and phrases. Then write the subject and the main idea on the lines below.

from Sarah, Plain and Tall by Patricia MacLachlan

The sheep made Sarah smile. She sank her fingers into their thick, coarse wool. She talked to them, running with the lambs, letting them suck on her fingers. She named them after her favorite aunts, Harriet and Mattie and Lou. She lay down in the field beside them and sang "Summer Is Icumen in," her voice drifting over the meadow grasses, carried by the wind.

What is the subject of the paragraph? the sheep and Sarah

What is the author saying about this subject? Sarah loves the sheep.

Step 4: Find support for the main idea.

Good writers support their main ideas with strong facts and details. A Main Idea Organizer can help you see how the main idea and details work together in a paragraph.

Directions: Complete these organizers. The first is for *Volcano*. The second is for *Sarah, Plain and Tall*. Write the subject for each one. List details that support the main idea. Then, sum it all up by writing the main idea for each paragraph in the main idea box.

Main Idea Organizer

Title: Volcano

Subject: Mount St. Helens

Detail #1	Detail #2	Detail #3
Molten rock forced its way to the surface.	The lava poured out and hardened.	Sprays of lava burst into the sky and hardened.

Main Idea: Mount St. Helens was built by many eruptions.

Main Idea Organizer

Title: Sarah, Plain and Tall

Subject: the sheep and Sarah

Detail #1	Detail #2	Detail #3
She runs her hands through their wool.	She names them after her favorite aunts.	She sings to them.

Main Idea: Sarah has a great relationship with the sheep. She loves them.

Reading Social Studies

Social studies textbooks show you the world of the past and the world of today. Your job is to keep track of the facts, ideas, and terms discussed in each chapter. This reading plan can help.

Before Reading

When you open your social studies textbook, don't just dive headfirst into the reading! First, make a plan. A good plan will help you understand what you read. In fourth grade, you may be studying the history of your state. Here, you'll use the reading process and the strategy of using graphic organizers to help you read a social studies chapter called "States and Boundaries."

A Set a Purpose

When reading a social studies chapter, your purpose is to learn facts about the subject and how it connects to you personally.

• **To set your purpose, ask a question about the chapter title.**

Directions: Ask a question about the chapter "States and Boundaries." Then predict what the reading will be about. You will read to find the answer to your question.

My question: What do I need to know about states and boundaries?

My prediction: I think I'll find out what a state is and maybe the kinds of boundaries that separate one state from another.

Textbooks

B Preview

When you preview a textbook chapter, look for key information.

Directions: Run your eyes over the chapter "States and Boundaries."
Make some notes on this chart.

Preview Questions	My Notes
What is the title of the chapter?	"States and Boundaries"
Look at the Study Guide. What is the main idea of this chapter?	The 50 U.S. states are separated by political and natural boundaries. Each state belongs to one or more regions of the country.
What else did you notice in the Study Guide?	Goals for reading
What are the key terms in this chapter?	state, history, geography, political boundary, natural boundary, region
What are the subheads?	Your State and Its Boundaries; Regions
Are there pictures, maps, charts, or diagrams? What did you notice about them?	There are 2 maps: a map of all the states in the U.S. and a map of Ohio.
What are the questions at the end of the chapter about?	They ask about boundaries and regions.

Reading Social Studies ■

NAME ....

FOR USE WITH PAGES 58–73

1 States and Boundaries

Key Terms
• • • • • • • • • • • • • • • •
state
history
geography
political boundary
natural boundary
region

Study Guide

Main Idea: The fifty states in our country are separated by political and natural boundaries. Each state belongs to one or more regions of the country.

Goals: As you read, look for answers to these questions:
• How is history different from geography?
• How is a political boundary formed?
• How is a natural boundary formed?

What can you learn if you sit down and study a map of the United States? The first thing that you might discover is that our country is divided into fifty parts. Each of these parts is called a **state,** which is a political division of a country. As you know, each state in the United States has its own name and government. But together, the fifty states make up one united country, the United States of America.

Figure 1.1 The United States

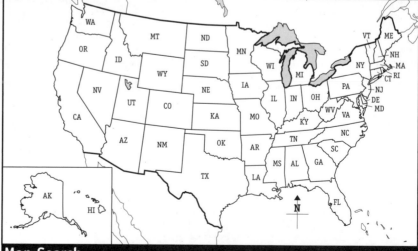

Map Search
Use the map to locate your state. Which states border yours?

Your State and Its Boundaries

To study your state, you must find out about its people. You must learn who the people are, where they live, and how they make a living. In addition, you need to understand the **history** and **geography** of your state. History is the study of the past. Geography is the study of the earth and how humans use it.

If you look at the map again on page 25, you'll notice that heavy black lines outline each state. These boundary lines show where one state ends and another begins. A line made by people to separate one state or country from another is called a **political boundary.**

Stop and Record

Make some notes in the "Political Boundary" section of your Web (page 28).

Some states or countries are separated from each other by **natural boundaries.** A natural boundary can be a lake, river, mountain range, or other type of land form. In some states, the political boundary line follows the natural boundary line of a river. For example, look at the southern half of Ohio. The political boundary line follows the natural boundary line of the Ohio River (see Figure 1.2). Can you find other states in which a political boundary line follows the natural boundary line of a river?

Figure 1.2 Ohio

Stop and Record

Make some notes in the "Natural Boundary" section of your Web (page 28).

Regions

When you study states, you can begin by looking at regions. A **region** is an area of the country whose parts have one or more characteristics in common. For example, the Northeast region of the United States includes the states of Pennsylvania, New York, New Jersey, Connecticut, Rhode Island, Massachusetts, New Hampshire, Vermont, and Maine. This region of the country shares a similar climate and a common history. Many states in the Northeast border the Atlantic Ocean. The ocean attracts summer visitors for swimming, boating, and fishing. Fishing and shipbuilding are important industries in some states in the Northeast. The ocean also helped make New York City an important port for worldwide trade.

Regions are different from each other for lots of reasons. They might be different because of the land itself. One area of a state might be dry and flat, while another is wet and marshy. They can also be different because of natural vegetation. These are the plants that grow in an area without the help of people. They might be different because of the industry in that region. Some states in the country belong to two or more regions. For example, a single state might belong to a mountain region, a farm region, and a manufacturing region.

Stop and Record

Make some notes in the "Region" section of your Web (page 28).

Check Point

1. How are political boundaries and natural boundaries similar? How are they different?

2. What are regions and how are they formed?

C Plan

Textbook chapters are chock-full of information. You need a plan that can help you understand and remember what you've learned.

• Use graphic organizers to keep track of key facts and details.

During Reading

Now go back and read "States and Boundaries."

D Read with a Purpose

A Web can help you keep related facts and details together.

Directions: Make notes on this Web as you read.

Web

Political Boundary

line made by people to separate one

state or country from another

Example: the state line that

separates California from Nevada

Natural Boundary

a landform that separates states

or countries

Examples: lake, river, mountain

range

"States and Boundaries"

Region

an area of the country whose parts have one or more

characteristics in common

Example: the Northeast

NAME ....

FOR USE WITH PAGES 58–73

Using the Strategy

A Web is just one way of organizing your notes on a social studies chapter. There are other graphic organizers that work just as well.

• **Key Word Notes can help you organize the main ideas from each chapter.**

Directions: Find the key words in "States and Boundaries." Make notes on each key word in the chart below.

Key Word Notes

Key Words	Notes
state	There are fifty states in the U.S.
	A state is a political division of a country.
history	History is the study of the past.
geography	Geography is the study of the earth and how humans use it.
political boundary	A political boundary is a line made by people to separate two states or countries.
natural boundary	Some states and countries are separated by natural boundaries.
	A natural boundary could be a lake, river, or mountain range.
	In some places, the political boundary line follows the natural boundary line.
region	A region is an area of the country whose parts have one or more characteristics in common.
	A single state can be part of several regions, such as a mountain region, a farm region, and a manufacturing region.

Understanding How Social Studies Textbooks Are Organized

Many social studies chapters open with a study guide or goals box. Here is the one from the chapter you just read.

Key Terms
• • • • • • • • • • • • • •
state
history
geography
political boundary
natural boundary
region

Study Guide

Main Idea: The fifty states in our country are separated by political and natural boundaries. Each state belongs to one or more regions of the country.

Goals: As you read, look for answers to these questions:
• How is history different from geography?
• How is a political boundary formed?
• How is a natural boundary formed?

Directions: Answer the questions under "Goals" in the Study Guide. Then define the key terms.

Goals

1. How is history different from geography? History is the study of the past. Geography is the study of the earth and how we use it.

2. How is a political boundary formed? It is formed by people who want to divide one state or country from another.

3. How is a natural boundary formed? It is formed by nature.

4. What is a region? A region is a part of the country with one or more characteristics in common.

◄ **Definitions of Key Terms**

state a political division of a country

history the study of the past

geography the study of the earth and how we use it

political boundary a line made by people to separate one state or country from

another

natural boundary a boundary that occurs naturally, such as a lake, river, mountain

range, or other landform

region an area of the country whose parts have one or more features in common

E Connect

When you make a connection to a text, you ask yourself questions such as, "What do I think about this?" or "What do I already know about this?"

- **Making a connection to a social studies text can make the facts and details seem more real to you.**

NAME ....

Directions: Answer the questions on these sticky notes.

Connection Questions

What state do you live in?

Pennsylvania

What states border your state?

New Jersey, Maryland,

Delaware, New York, Ohio,

West Virginia

What rivers and lakes are in your state?

Allegheny River, Delaware

River, Lake Erie

What region of the country do you live in?

Northeast, Great Lakes,

Manufacturing Belt, Dairy

Belt

After Reading

After you finish reading, think about what you've learned.

F Pause and Reflect

Return to your purpose question. Can you answer it now?

● **Ask yourself, "Have I met my purpose?"**

Directions: Write your purpose question from page 23 on the line below. Then answer it.

My question: What do I need to know about states and boundaries?

My answer: I need to find out more about regions. I'm not sure what the different regions are and what region of the country my state falls in.

© GREAT SOURCE. ALL RIGHTS RESERVED.

NAME ....

 G **Reread**

The rereading strategy of finding causes and effects can help you make links between ideas in social studies.

- **At the rereading stage, create a Cause-Effect Organizer.**

Directions: Complete this Cause-Effect Organizer. Refer to your notes and the selection on pages 25–27.

Cause-Effect Organizer

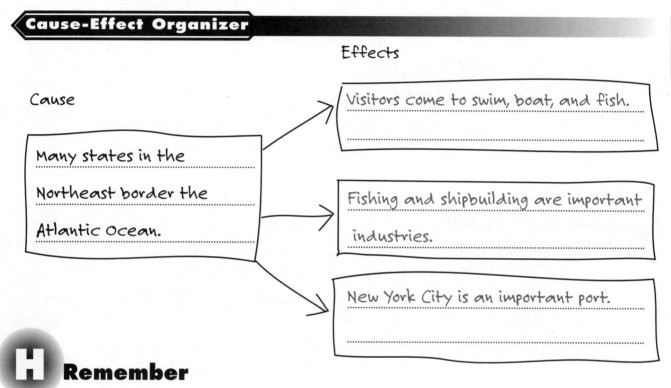

Effects

Cause

Many states in the Northeast border the Atlantic Ocean.

Visitors come to swim, boat, and fish.

Fishing and shipbuilding are important industries.

New York City is an important port.

H **Remember**

It's important to remember what you learn in social studies.

- **Making a personal connection to the information can help you remember it.**

Directions: Write a Journal Entry about your state. Write at least three facts or details.

Journal Entry

I live in Pennsylvania. It is bordered by New York, New Jersey, Delaware, Maryland, West Virginia, and Ohio. I live in the Dairy Belt region of Pennsylvania. There are lots of dairy farms here. They produce milk, cheese, sour cream, and other products.

Reading Science

If science is hard for you, you might want to change the way you read the textbook. Choose some strategies that can help you get more information from every page. Practice here.

Before Reading

Use the reading process and the strategy of note-taking to help you read and understand a science textbook chapter on the seven continents and how they were formed.

 Set a Purpose

Your purpose for reading science is to learn about the subject. You will need to learn the key facts or details about the subject.

- **To set your purpose, ask a question about the subject of the chapter.**

Directions: Write your purpose for reading "Understanding Pangaea" here. Then make a prediction about the chapter. What do you expect to learn?

My purpose: What is Pangaea? What are the most important facts I need to learn about Pangaea?

....

I think the reading will be about: I'm not sure what Pangaea is, but I think it might have something to do with the continents. I'll need to preview carefully since the subject is unfamiliar to me.

....

....

NAME

B Preview

The reason you preview is to find out the subject of the chapter and get an idea of what you will be learning.

Directions: Preview the science chapter that follows. Place a check beside each text feature after you look at it. Then make some notes about your preview on the table below.

- ☑ Title and subheadings
- ☑ Guide for Reading
- ☑ Words in boldface
- ☑ Photos, maps, diagrams, and so on
- ☑ First and last paragraphs

Preview Chart

The titles and headings tell me . . .
The chapter is about Pangaea.
There is a puzzle to be solved.
Someone named Wegener is involved.
I will learn about plate tectonics.

I saw these boldfaced words . . .	
continents	fossils
supercontinent	plate tectonics
Pangaea	plates
theory	

"Understanding Pangaea"

The Guide for Reading, maps, and diagrams tell me . . .
Pangaea has something to do with the continents and how they move.
I also see a map that shows the earth's "plates."

The first and last paragraphs tell me . . .
The seven continents look like a puzzle. Pangaea no longer exists, but there may be a new one some time in the future.

Chapter 2

Understanding Pangaea

A "Puzzle" to Solve

Take a careful look at a map of the world (Figure 2.1). Do you notice that the shapes of the seven **continents** (Africa, Antarctica, Asia, Australia, Europe, North America, and South America) seem to resemble pieces of a jigsaw puzzle? What if you were to move some of those pieces around? You might find that a few almost fit together.

GUIDE FOR READING

GOALS
1. Learn about Pangaea.
2. Learn the theory of plate tectonics.
3. Understand how Pangaea became the seven continents we know today.

KEY TERMS

continent	theory
supercontinent	fossil
Pangaea	plate tectonics
plate	

ACTIVITY AT HOME

Trace a picture of the seven continents on a sheet of paper. Then cut each continent out and form your own Pangaea.

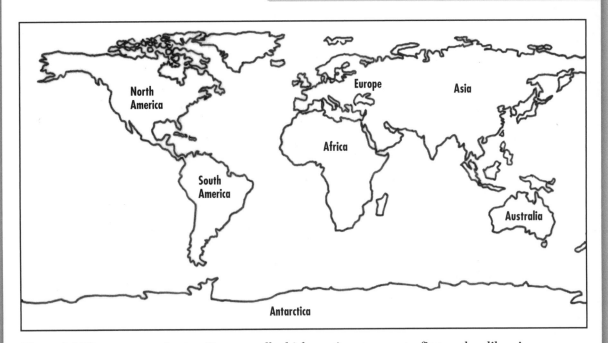

Figure 2.1 The seven continents. Can you tell which continents seem to fit together like pieces of a puzzle?

In the early 1900s, a German scientist named Alfred Wegener noticed this same thing—that the seven continents of the world looked like puzzle pieces. After some careful study, he proposed that the continents were long ago a part of one huge landmass—a **supercontinent**—that was surrounded by a single ocean (see Figure 2.2).

Wegener's Theory

Wegener named this supercontinent **Pangaea** (pan-JEE-uh), which is the Greek word for "all Earth." To support his **theory** that Pangaea had once existed, Wegener began studying the **fossils**—remains of living things—discovered on either side of the Atlantic Ocean. He noticed that these fossils were very similar, as if they had all lived together on one body of land.

Figure 2.2 The supercontinent Pangaea

When Wegener introduced the idea of Pangaea to the scientific community, he was laughed at. Scientists around the world poked fun at his ideas and said that it was impossible for huge masses of solid rock to break apart and drift across the globe. Soon, Wegener's theory of Pangaea was all but forgotten.

Pangaea and Plate Tectonics

In the 1960s, a Canadian scientist named J. Tuzo Wilson reopened the case for Pangaea. Wilson believed that Wegener was on the right track when he said that the seven continents were once one huge landmass. Pangaea, Wilson said, really *did* exist.

What Wegener was wrong about, however, was his theory that the continents had just drifted on their own into their current positions. The continents did move, Wilson said, but they moved as a result of **plate tectonics.**

Plate tectonics is the theory that the Earth's crust is made up of about 30 huge **plates** (blocks) that are always very slowly moving. As the plates move, the oceans and landmasses on the surface of the earth change in shape, size, and position (see Figure 2.3).

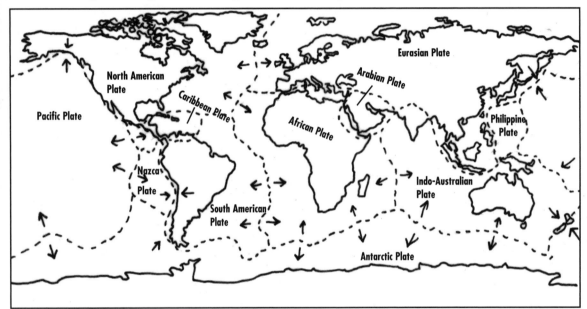

For example, scientists now know that the Atlantic Ocean grows around 2 cm. wider each year as the tectonic plates on either side of the Atlantic move apart. Although 2 cm. a year doesn't sound like much, think of how much larger the Atlantic Ocean will be in another 100 million years. It's possible that in the far-off future, the Atlantic, and not the Pacific, will be the largest ocean on earth. It's also possible that one day all of the continents will once again be joined together as one supercontinent—a "new" Pangaea.

Figure 2.3
Scientists say the Earth's surface is made up of about thirty plates.

Plan

Now make a plan. Choose a strategy that can help you read, understand, and remember what you've learned.

• **Use the strategy of note-taking to get more from a science text.**

Good readers take notes before, during, and after a reading.

During Reading

Now do a careful reading of "Understanding Pangaea."

D Read with a Purpose

Keep in mind that your purpose is to find out about the subject.

Directions: Make notes on this Web as you read.

Web

A supercontinent

Broke apart into seven continents

Pangaea

Plate tectonics explained why the continents moved.

Fossils were similar on both sides of Atlantic.

Using the Strategy

There are many different ways to take notes. Choose the tool that's best for you. Since science is partly the study of cause and effect, many readers find it helps to take notes on a Cause-Effect Organizer.

- **A Cause-Effect Organizer helps you see the relationship between several events.**

<u>Directions</u>: Complete this organizer by noting the cause of each event. Refer to your notes as needed.

Cause-Effect Organizer

Causes

Effects

| The continents were once part of one large landmass that broke apart. | ▶ | The seven continents look like they could fit together like puzzle pieces. |

| Animals once all lived together on one body of land. | ▶ | The same fossils are found on both sides of the Atlantic Ocean. |

| Plates in the earth move and shift over time. | ▶ | Pangaea broke apart into separate continents. |

| Tectonic plates on both sides of the Atlantic Ocean are moving apart. | ▶ | The Atlantic Ocean is growing wider every year. |

Write causes in these boxes. A cause answers the question "why?"

40

Understanding How Science Texts Are Organized

Often a science text will tell the steps in a process. When you read a textbook, it helps to keep track of the steps in the process described.

Directions: Make Process Notes about Pangaea.

Process Notes

Tectonic plates on the surface of the Earth shift back and forth.

Pangaea moves as the plates move.

▼

Pangaea breaks apart.

▼ Write what happens eventually to Pangaea here.

Continents take different positions.

▼ Tell what happens to the seven continents here.

Continents and oceans continue to change as plates continue to shift.

Tell what is still happening to the continents and oceans here.

E Connect

Connecting to a science reading makes it easier to understand.

• **Ask yourself, "What is most interesting about the reading?" or "How do these ideas explain what I see?"**

Directions: Write your reactions to the Pangaea chapter.

This is what I found most interesting: I had no idea that the continents were once connected. That's so strange to think of.

Textbooks

After Reading

Be sure you understand what you've read before moving on to another chapter or assignment.

F Pause and Reflect

Return to your reading purpose and ask yourself what you've learned.

• **After you finish reading, ask, "Did I meet my purpose?"**

Directions: Answer *yes* or *no* to these questions.

Do you know the main topic of the chapter? yes

Can you explain the key terms? yes

Do the graphics, pictures, and captions make sense? yes

Could you explain the topic in your own words? maybe

G Reread

If you can't answer *yes* to each question, you need to do some rereading.

• **The rereading strategy of paraphrasing can help you understand information.**

Directions: Paraphrase, or tell in your own words, what you've learned about Pangaea.

Paraphrase

A long time ago, the seven continents of the world were all joined together like pieces in a puzzle. The landmass was called Pangaea. Over time, Pangaea broke apart. Plate tectonics caused it to break. Today, the earth's plates continue to shift. This means that the continents continue to change shape and position.

NAME ....

Remember

Drawing helps you remember what you've learned.

• To remember a science chapter, make a sketch.

<u>**Directions:**</u> In box #1, draw Pangaea. In box #2, draw what the world looks like today. In box #3, draw what you think the world will look like a hundred thousand years from now.

1. Then

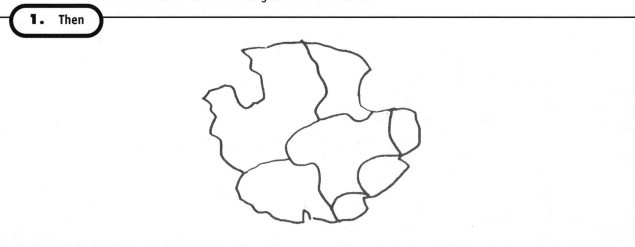

2. Now

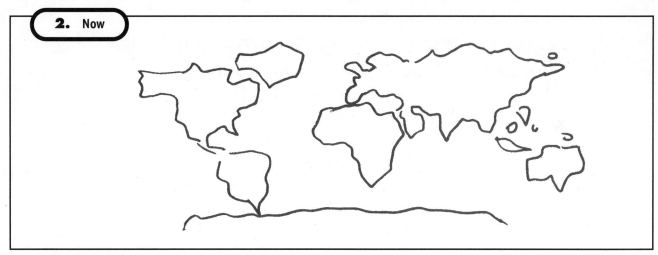

3. In the future

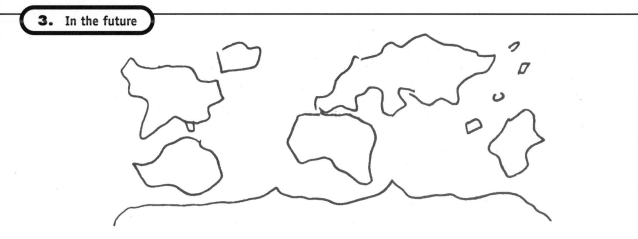

Textbooks

Reading Math

Reading counts in every subject you take, including math. In math class, you read numbers, symbols, word problems, definitions of key terms, and much more. Good reading strategies can help you learn math.

Before Reading

Practice reading a math book here. Use the strategy of visualizing to help you understand what you read.

A Set a Purpose

Begin by setting your purpose. Turn the chapter title into a question and make that your purpose for reading.

- **To set your purpose, ask a question about the chapter title.**

Directions: Write your purpose for reading a math chapter called "Telling Time and Reading a Calendar." Then say what you think will be easiest and hardest about this chapter.

My purpose: What do I need to know about telling time and reading a calendar?

The easiest part will be: the calendar part. I'm good at that.

The hardest part will be: I might have a little trouble with the
telling time part. Sometimes I get mixed up.

 B Preview

It is important to preview a math text before you begin reading. Look for the lesson's subject, directions, examples, and any explanations.

• Use a K-W-L Chart for your preview notes.

Directions: Preview the two math pages that follow. Look for the items on this checklist. Then make notes on this K-W-L Chart. Fill in the "What I Know" and "What I Want to Know" columns now. Fill in the "What I Learned" column after you read the chapter.

◀ Preview Checklist ▶

✔ the chapter title and any subtitles

✔ key terms

✔ practice problems

◀ K-W-L Chart ▶

What I **K**now	What I **W**ant to Know	What I **L**earned
Sample answer: I know how to read a calendar, and I can tell time sometimes, but I get mixed up with a.m. and p.m.	When to use a.m. and when to use p.m. How to write dates	You use a.m. for times before noon and p.m. for times after noon. A calendar can tell you what day a date falls on. You can write dates using ordinal numbers. For example, June 8, 1974 = 6/8/74
⟨Write what you already know here.⟩	⟨Write what you need to find out about the subject here.⟩	⟨Make notes in this section after your careful reading.⟩

Lesson
11 Telling Time and Reading a Calendar

Goals
- Learn a.m. and p.m. and the difference between them.
- Understand days and dates on a calendar.

Key Terms
- a.m.
- p.m.
- ordinal numbers

Learn About It: **A.M. and P.M.**

An hour hand goes around a clock two times each day. It goes around once for the **a.m.** hours, which are before noon. It also goes around once for the **p.m.** hours, which are after noon.

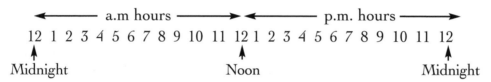

←———— a.m hours ————→ ←———— p.m. hours ————→

12 1 2 3 4 5 6 7 8 9 10 11 12 1 2 3 4 5 6 7 8 9 10 11 12

↑   ↑   ↑

Midnight   Noon   Midnight

TIP: Thinking of a timeline like this one can help you decide whether a time is in the a.m. or p.m. hours.

Practice
Directions Use the timeline above to answer these questions.
1. What are two things you do in the a.m. hours?
2. What are two things you do in the p.m. hours?

Directions Write a.m. or p.m. to complete each sentence.
3. I have breakfast at 7
4. Every afternoon my sister goes swimming at 2:20
5. Father made lunch for us at 11:45
6. My favorite evening TV show comes on at 8

Draw a timeline to help you answer question 3.

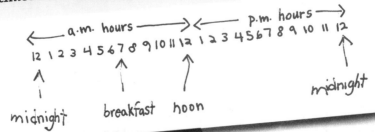

Learn About It: **Days and Dates on a Calendar**

To talk about dates on a calendar, you need to know the order of the days and weeks. For example:

In 2004, January 11 is on Sunday.

January 31 is on Saturday.

There are twelve months in a year. You can use **ordinal numbers,** or numbers used to tell order, to describe the months. For example, August is the 8th month.

You can write the date like this:

August 8, 2004

or like this: *8/8/04   or   8/8/2004*

| January 2004 | | | | | | |
S	M	T	W	T	F	S
				1	2	3
4	5	6	7	8	9	10
11	12	13	14	15	16	17
18	19	20	21	22	23	24
25	26	27	28	29	30	31

This is how I know that January 11 is on a Sunday. I find 11 on the calendar. I run my finger up to the days at the top. I see that 11 is written under Sunday. So January 11 is a Sunday.

Textbooks

Practice

Directions Use the January 2004 calendar to answer these questions.

1. Jin has a doctor's appointment on the third Monday of the month. What is the date of Jin's appointment?
2. Seth will take the dog to the vet on the last day of the month. What is the day and date of the vet appointment?

Directions Name the month.

3. the sixth
4. the ninth
5. the twelfth

Directions Write these dates another way.

6. 10/4/02
7. June 16, 1991
8. 1/24/94
9. March 11, 2001

C Plan

Your next step is to make a plan for reading the math chapter. Choose a strategy that can help you meet your reading purpose.

- **Use the strategy of visualizing and thinking aloud to help you understand what you are reading.**

When you visualize, you make a mental picture of the problem. When you think aloud, you talk your way through the problem step by step.

During Reading

Now go back and do a careful reading of the two math pages.

D Read with a Purpose

Keep in mind your purpose for reading. Remember that you want to learn about telling time and reading calendars. Make notes on the sticky notes. Then complete the "What I Learned" part of the K-W-L Chart on page 45.

Using the Strategy

Directions: On the lines below, think aloud about how you would use the January calendar on page 47 to solve this problem.

1. Jin has a doctor's appointment on the third Monday of the month. What is the date of Jin's appointment?

Think Aloud

To find the answer, first I'll look across the day line at the top of the

calendar until I come to the Monday column. Then I'll run my finger down

the Monday column, counting as I go. When I get to the third Monday, I'll check

the date and find out that it's the 19th.

Understanding How Math Texts Are Organized

Most math chapters open with a study guide like the one below. In most cases, the study guide box will list the goals and key terms of the chapter.

Goals
- Learn a.m. and p.m. and the difference between them.
- Understand days and dates on a calendar.

Key Terms
- a.m.
- p.m.
- ordinal numbers

After you read a math chapter, go back to the study guide box. Check to see that you've met each goal and learned the key terms.

Directions: Answer these questions using notes from your reading.

What is a.m.? *the hours before noon*

What is p.m.? *the hours after noon*

How are they different? *One is for morning, and the other is for afternoon and evening.*

What are ordinal numbers? *numbers used to tell order*

What is the ordinal number for June? *6*

Textbooks

E Connect

Making a personal connection to a math problem can help you solve it.

> • **Ask yourself, "What does this have to do with me?"**

Directions: Write your daily schedule in Column 1. Circle a.m. or p.m. Write your birthday in ordinal numbers in Column 2.

Daily Schedule	My Birthday	
I get up at 7 (a.m.) p.m.	May 7, 1992	month, day, year
I eat lunch at 1 a.m. (p.m.)	5/7/92	in ordinal numbers
I do my homework at 7 a.m. (p.m.)	Note: All answers are examples only.	
I go to bed at 9 a.m. (p.m.)		

After Reading

When you finish reading, take some time to think about the chapter. Often you will need to review what you've read to really learn it.

F Pause and Reflect

Look again at page 44. Reread your reading purpose.

> • **At this point, ask yourself, "Did I meet my purpose?"**

Directions: Check *Yes* or *No* in response to each question.

Checklist	Yes	No
I understand the key terms.	✔	
I can explain what each term means.	✔	
I can answer the practice problems.		✔

Reread

Sometimes one reading of a math chapter is not enough. You may need to reread some parts. Try a different strategy when you reread.

• Use the strategy of note-taking when you reread.

Directions: Read the key words and topics in the left column. Make notes about them in the right column.

Key Word Notes

Key Words or Topics	My Notes
a.m.	the hours before noon
p.m.	the hours after noon
examples	I wake up at 6 a.m. I go to bed at 9 p.m.
ordinal numbers	numbers used to tell order
example	7/4/1776

Remember

Don't turn the page in your math text until you're sure you remember what you've already learned.

• Creating sample tests can help you remember math material.

Directions: Make a sample math test for a friend to take. Write one problem for telling time and one problem for reading a calendar. (Look at the math problems on pages 46–47 if you need help.)

Sample Test

1. Telling time: What time do you go to school?

2. Reading a calendar: What is the date of the last day of this year?

Focus on Word Problems

Math word problems require thinking and planning. Here is a four-step plan that can help.

Step 1: Read.

Begin by reading the problem several times until it makes sense.

Directions: Read this word problem. Underline the main question. Tell how you decided what key facts to look for.

Sample Word Problem

A family of two adults and four children went to the movies last night. Adult tickets cost $8.25 each. Kids' tickets cost $4.75 each. Every child bought a box of popcorn for $3.00 per box. <u>How much altogether did the family spend on tickets and refreshments at the movies last night?</u>

Think Aloud

The main question is: "How much altogether did the family spend on tickets and refreshments?" So I need to know how many people are in the family, how much tickets cost, and how much refreshments cost.

Step 2: Plan.

Next, choose a strategy. Visualizing works well with word problems.

Directions: Make a sketch that shows the problem.

$8.25 $8.25 $4.75 $4.75 $4.75 $4.75 $3.00 $3.00 $3.00 $3.00

Step 3: Solve.

Next, use your notes and sketch to solve the problem.

Directions: Write a think-aloud. Then solve the problem.

Think Aloud

To answer the question, I'll have to do a lot of multiplying. There were 2 adult tickets, so that's $8.25 times 2. There were 4 kids' tickets, so that's $4.75 times 4. There were 4 boxes of popcorn, so that's $3.00 times 4. Then I'll add up all those totals to get the grand total.

$8.25 × 2 = $16.50 $4.75 × 4 = $19.00

$3.00 × 4 = $12.00 $16.50 + $19.00 + $12.00 = $47.50

Step 4: Check.

Every test-taker makes mistakes. This is why you must always check your work. Once again, thinking aloud can help.

Directions: A good way to check your work is to do it another way. Write a think-aloud that tells how you'd solve this problem another way.

Think Aloud

You could add up all the individual costs instead of multiplying.

$8.25 + $8.25 + $4.75 + $4.75 + $4.75 + $4.75 = $35.50.

$3.00 + $3.00 + $3.00 + $3.00 = $12.00.

$35.50 + $12.00 = $47.50.

Focus on Questions

Questions, questions, questions. You can't get away from them—especially if you're reading a textbook.

Step 1: Read the question.

First read each question several times until you know what it's asking.

Directions: Read the two questions below. Underline key words and information.

Population Growth

Over 6 billion people live in the world today. For thousands of years, human population grew very slowly. In 1650, there were about 550 million people in the world. By 1850, two hundred years later, the population had doubled to just over 1 billion. Since then, the population has increased very rapidly. The population in Europe grew quickly in the 1700s as death rates dropped. In the 1990s, however, most population increases were in Asia, Africa, and Latin America. People began to live longer on these continents due to fewer famines, better health care, and better water supplies and sanitation.

1. What was the world population in 1650? What is it today?
2. **CRITICAL THINKING** What is one possible reason why death rates declined in Europe in the 1700s?

Step 2: Think about the question.

Next decide what each question is asking.

Directions: Write what the questions are asking you to find.

Question 1 is asking me for facts—the world population in 1650 and today.

Question 2 is asking me to tell why death rates went down in Europe in the 1700s.

Step 3: Gather information.

You'll find answers to factual questions in your textbook. Identify the key words in the question, and skim the text to find those key words. To answer critical thinking questions, combine information from the text with what you already know.

Directions: Explain where you will look for information for the two questions.

For question #1, I will skim the paragraph, looking for the key words "1650" and "today."

For question #2, I will go back to the paragraph and skim for reasons why the death rate might drop.

Step 4: Answer.

Use the information you've gathered to answer the questions.

Directions: Read the "Population Growth" passage on page 54. Answer questions 1 and 2.

1. The population was 550 million in 1650. Today it is more than 6 billion.

2. Students only need to give one reason. Possible reasons include discoveries in science that led to better treatments for disease, better sanitation, better farming methods, and other inventions that improved living conditions.

Step 5: Check.

Be sure you have in fact answered the question. To check your work, reread both the question and the answer.

Directions: Exchange books with a partner. Check to see that your partner has answered the questions. Make notes in the margin.

Textbooks

Reading a Magazine Article

Sometimes you'll read a magazine just for fun. Other times you need to read a magazine article for a school assignment. In that case, the reading process and the strategy of questioning the author can help.

Before Reading

Use the reading process and the strategy of questioning the author to help you understand and respond to an article about the *Hindenburg*.

A Set a Purpose

To set your purpose, ask yourself about the topic of the magazine article. Also ask why that topic is important.

- **Use key words from the title of the article to form a reading purpose.**

Directions: Write your purpose for reading the magazine article "The Mighty *Hindenburg*: A Hydrogen Horror." Then tell what you already know about the topic.

My purpose: I want to find out what the <u>Hindenburg</u> was and why it is important to

learn about.

What I know about the topic: I've heard about the <u>Hindenburg</u>. I think it was some

type of blimp that crashed.

NAME ....

 Preview

When you preview, keep an eye out for the **subject** of the article. Look for clues in the title, any photographs or illustrations, headings or large type, and the first and last paragraphs.

Directions: Preview the magazine article that follows. Write your preview notes on this chart.

My Preview Notes

The title of the article is: The Mighty Hindenburg: A Hydrogen Horror

What I noticed about the art:	What I learned from the headings:
There is a blimp with a ball of fire behind it.	The Hindenburg had a terrible flaw.
I think the blimp has exploded.	There was a final trip.
	There was a fire.
	The passengers and crew were terrified.
	The incident taught a lesson.
What I learned from the first and last paragraphs:	What I think the subject of this article is:
The Hindenburg was a big airship. On the trip, there were 36 passengers and 61 crewmembers. After the Hindenburg disaster, safety was very important for air travel.	Some terrible fire involving the Hindenburg.

Nonfiction

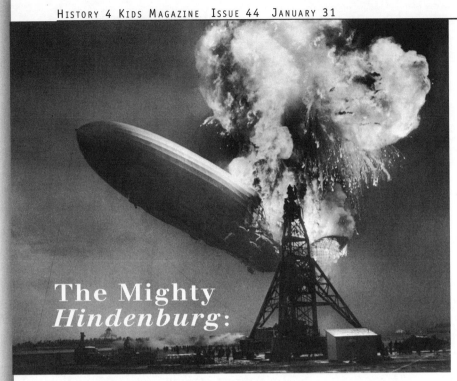

HISTORY 4 KIDS MAGAZINE   ISSUE 44   JANUARY 31

The Mighty Hindenburg:

The *Hindenburg* explodes on its landing approach in Lakehurst, New Jersey

A HYDROGEN HORROR

The huge airship rose softly into the evening sky. Passengers stood at the windows and waved goodbye to the people down below. Others sat in cozy chairs and drank champagne. The 36 passengers and 61 crewmembers felt very lucky. They were travelling on the *Hindenburg,* the most magnificent dirigible* ever made.

Stop and Question

Why does the writer open the article with this little story about the **Hindenburg?** (Write your answer on page 61.)

*dirigible — A dirigible is an airship or "blimp."

The *Hindenburg* was built in Germany in the early 1930s. Its first trip was in April 1936. Soon the big airship was making many trips back and forth between Germany and the United States. It seemed like everyone wanted a chance to fly in the *Hindenburg.*

A TERRIBLE FLAW

Believe it or not, the *Hindenburg* was longer than three football fields! It could fly 84 miles an hour and could carry over a hundred passengers. With the help of four propellers and a huge engine, the *Hindenburg* was able to make the trip from Germany to the U.S. in just three short days.

"The Mighty Hindenburg," continued

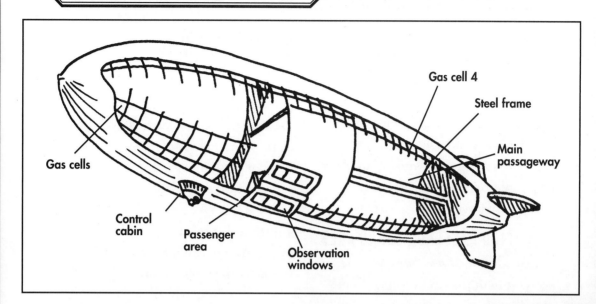

Gas cell 4

Steel frame

Main passageway

Gas cells

Control cabin

Passenger area

Observation windows

But the *Hindenburg* had a terrible flaw. It was powered by hydrogen, which is a gas that catches fire very easily. Some people worried that a dropped match or a spark from a cooking stove would set the airship on fire.

THE FINAL TRIP

In May of 1937, the *Hindenburg* lifted off from Frankfurt, Germany, for its eleventh trip across the ocean. Guiding the ship was Captain Max Pruss, a German World War I fighter pilot. In the passenger cabins, men and women drank champagne and ate the finest food money could buy.

Three days after lifting off from Frankfurt, Pruss guided the ship over New York City. He was heading straight on course toward the landing strip in Lakehurst, New Jersey. The trip had been a fairly easy one. Still, Captain Pruss was looking forward to landing.

Stop and Question

Why does the author give so much detail about the May 1937 trip? (Question your answer on page 61.)

FIREBALL!

At 6:00 that evening, the *Hindenburg* glided into position above Lakehurst Airfield. On the ground, hundreds of people stood waiting for the ship to land. In the group were dozens of newspaper and radio reporters who were eager to report on the journey.

Inside the rear of the ship, two crewmen noticed something that made them fall to their knees in horror. A small blue and yellow fireball was spinning and turning inside cell number 4 of the hydrogen compartment!

In the blink of an eye, the small ball became a huge tower of orange

"The Mighty Hindenburg," continued

and red flames. A freight train of fire began speeding its way through the middle of the ship. Huge flames licked at all sides of the craft. Smoke rose in a mushroom cloud overhead. Within seconds, the *Hindenburg* began to sink. Hundreds of people on the ground began diving for cover.

TERRIFIED PASSENGERS AND CREW

Inside the *Hindenburg*, people were screaming and crying. Some passengers tried to jump out the windows, but the *Hindenburg* was sinking too fast. Suddenly, the tail of the ship hit the ground. A few passengers were sucked into the fire that raged in the tail.

Stop and Question

Why does the author want us to visualize, or picture, the burning craft? (Write your answer on page 61.)

Moments after the ship settled on the ground, passengers began running for their lives. They jumped through walls of fire and pushed their way through burning rubble. People on the ground at Lakehurst ran to help. Some even ran into the fire in order to drag more passengers from the flames.

Miraculously, 62 passengers and crew made it safely out of the ship.

A LESSON FOR ALL

In a mere 32 seconds, the *Hindenburg* was a heap of smoking garbage. Reporters who had seen the tragedy sent pictures and stories of the burning *Hindenburg* to newspapers all over the world. One radio reporter, Herb Morrison of radio station WLS in Chicago, gave a minute-by-minute live description of the tragedy, which was broadcast the next day. The horror of the event could clearly be heard in his shocked voice. Later, survivors were interviewed on the radio as well. A horrified public demanded answers.

Unfortunately, no one has ever figured out what caused the *Hindenburg* to go up in flames. Some say that an electrical spark in the air caused the hydrogen inside the craft to catch fire.

Even if the cause remains a mystery, the result is quite clear. The *Hindenburg* disaster taught the world an important lesson about flying. From that point on, safety— and not luxury—would be the most important part of air travel.

Stop and Question

Why did the author end the article with information about the lesson learned? (Write your answer on page 61.)

C Plan

After your preview, make a reading plan.

• Use the strategy of questioning the author to help you get more from a magazine article.

During Reading

Now do a careful reading of "The Mighty *Hindenburg*: A Hydrogen Horror." Stop along the way to ask questions of the author.

D Read with a Purpose

Keep in mind your purpose for reading. Remember that you're looking for information about the topic and why it is important.

Directions: Write answers to your author questions here.

Questioning the Author

Page 58

Why does the author open the article with this little story about the <u>Hindenburg</u>?

It helps us understand what it was like to take a trip on the <u>Hindenburg</u>.

Page 59

Why does the author give so much detail about the May 1937 trip?

This is probably the trip during which the fire started.

Page 60

Why does the author want us to visualize, or picture, the burning craft?

All these details help us feel like we're seeing the crash. This makes

the article more interesting.

Page 60

Why did the author end the article with information about the lesson learned?

Sample answers: It's an interesting way to connect this event in the past to

today. It tells us why it's important to know about the <u>Hindenburg</u>.

Using the Strategy

Questioning the author means thinking about **why** the author wrote these words. This means that you have to evaluate what the article means.

- **Use a Double-entry Journal to record your thoughts and feelings about the article.**

Directions: Make notes on this Double-entry Journal.

Double-entry Journal

Quotes	My Thoughts and Feelings
"Passengers stood at the windows and waved goodbye to the people down below. Others sat in cozy chairs and drank champagne."	Sample responses: It really sounds nice.
"But the *Hindenburg* had a terrible flaw. It was powered by hydrogen, which is a gas that catches fire very easily."	They were dumb to build it!
"A freight train of fire began speeding its way through the middle of the ship."	I would have been scared.
"Miraculously, 62 passengers and crew made it safely out of the ship."	I can't believe so many people made it out alive.

Understanding How Magazine Articles Are Organized

Like news stories, many magazine articles answer the key questions *who, what, where, when, why,* and *how.*

Directions: Complete this 5 W's and H Organizer with information from the *Hindenburg* article.

5 W's and H Organizer

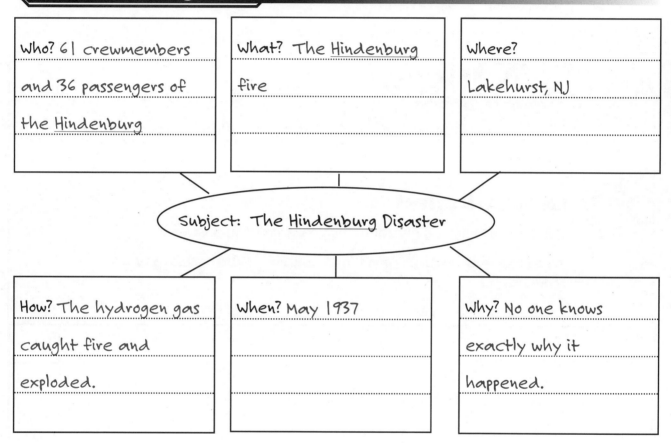

Who? 61 crewmembers and 36 passengers of the Hindenburg

What? The Hindenburg fire

Where? Lakehurst, NJ

Subject: The Hindenburg Disaster

How? The hydrogen gas caught fire and exploded.

When? May 1937

Why? No one knows exactly why it happened.

E Connect

It's important to connect with what you read in a magazine article.

- **Recording your reactions can help you process and remember what you've learned.**

Directions: Complete these statements.

Here's how I felt as I read the article: I felt suspense. I also felt worried. I could tell something bad was coming.

This is what I've learned: I've learned something about air travel of the past, and I'm grateful that this kind of airship is no longer used for travel.

After Reading

When you finish an article, take a moment to reflect on your original reading purpose.

F Pause and Reflect

Reread your purpose question and see if you can answer it.

- **To reflect on your purpose, ask yourself, "Did I meet my purpose?"**

Directions: Check *yes* or *no* to the items on this list.

Checklist	Yes	No
I have learned several important facts about the <u>Hindenburg</u>.	✔	
I understand why the topic is important.	✔	
I have evaluated the author's evidence.		✔

G Reread

Good readers know how important it is to evaluate the evidence the author presents.

- **Use the strategy of reading critically to help you decide if the evidence is reliable.**

NAME _____

Directions: Answer these questions about the *Hindenburg* article.

Critical Reading Chart

1. Is the main idea or viewpoint clear?	Yes. The Hindenburg was a terrible disaster.
2. What evidence is presented?	This article tells about the crash and the flawed construction of the ship.
3. Is the evidence convincing?	Yes. I feel I really understand why the Hindenburg crashed and what happened as a result.
4. Is there another side to the story?	I would like to hear from the people who built the Hindenburg. Why did they use a dangerous gas like hydrogen?

H Remember

Take what you learn from a magazine article and make it your own. This can help you remember what you've read.

• **To remember a magazine article, connect what you've read to your own life.**

Directions: Use the Internet or the library to find out more about the *Hindenburg* or another air disaster. List your research questions here.

Topic: Amelia Earhart

My Questions: (Sample provided)

1. Who was Amelia Earhart?

2. What did she do?

3. Where did she live and work?

4. When did she live?

5. Why is she important?

Nonfiction

Reading a News Story

When you want up-to-the-minute news, you pick up a newspaper or log on to the Internet. News stories tell you what's going on in your town and around the world. They also can help you form opinions and make decisions.

Before Reading

Sometimes you'll read a news story for fun. Sometimes you'll read one for a class assignment. In either case, the reading process and the strategy of summarizing can help.

A Set a Purpose

Your general purpose for reading a news story is to get the facts and figure out what they mean.

• **To set your purpose, take several words from the headline and turn them into a question.**

Directions: Write your purpose for reading "Hamilton Mets Face Their Toughest Opponent to Date" below. Then write some prereading questions about the article.

My purpose: I want to read this article to find out what happened when the

Mets faced their toughest opponent to date.

My questions: Examples: Who are the Mets? What sport do they play? Where did

the game take place? When did they play? Why was this the Mets' toughest

match ever?

NAME ....

 Preview

News stories are written for people who are in a hurry. Reporters know that readers want information *fast*. For this reason, you'll find the most important information in the first few paragraphs of the article, called "the lead."

Directions: Use this checklist to preview "Hamilton Mets Face Their Toughest Opponent to Date." Put a check mark next to each item after you look at it. Then make some notes about your preview in the Preview Chart below.

☑ Read the headline.

☑ Read the first paragraph.

☑ Skim the article, looking for repeated words.

☑ Look at any photos or captions.

Preview Chart

The headline tells me . . .	The first paragraph tells me . . .
The Hamilton Mets played a game, and it was tough.	The Hamilton Mets are a Little League team. Their home game yesterday was against Valley Stream. It was their hardest game to date.
I noticed these repeated words . . .	**The photos and captions tell me . . .**
inning, coach, scored, ball	that outfielder Ryan Lewis hit a double, and that the Hamilton Mets won the game.

Nonfiction

Hamilton Courier Times

LOCAL SPORTS EDITION · SUNDAY, MAY 11, 2003

HAMILTON METS FACE THEIR TOUGHEST OPPONENT TO DATE

BY THERESA SKOLNIK

After three tough wins against three tough teams, the Hamilton Mets Little League team was hoping for an easy home game yesterday afternoon against the Valley Stream team. What the Mets ended up playing, however, was the most challenging game of the season to date.

Stop and Record

Who and what is the news story about? When and where does the game take place? Make notes on your 5 W's and H Organizer (page 70).

From the very first pitch of the very first inning, Valley Stream showed they would be a tough opponent. Nine-year-old star pitcher Alex Scammel threw one strike after another and managed to strike out six of the Mets' star batters.

The Mets, who have shown themselves to be strong fielders in the past, seemed a little slow and a little tired yesterday. By the end of the fourth inning, Valley Stream had scored four runs, and the Mets had yet to make it to first base.

Mets outfielder Ryan Lewis pulls back for a double.

Mets coach Sam Shoemaker gathered his players on the bench and gave them the kind of pep talk that makes him the most popular coach in the league. Kids and parents alike listened as Shoemaker explained the line-up for the last two innings and gave batters tips on how to score against Valley Stream.

"Hamilton Mets Face Their Toughest Opponent to Date," continued

Stop and Record

Why are the Mets having trouble? Make notes on your 5 W's and H Organizer (page 70).

"At the end of the fourth inning," Coach Shoemaker explained later, "I realized our team was really discouraged. I told them that they could beat Valley Stream in the field

The Hamilton Mets celebrate another win.

and up at bat—but that they'd have to play as a *team*."

Coach Shoemaker's words of encouragement proved to be exactly what the Mets needed. The next inning, Mets outfielder Ryan Lewis hit a double and stole third. Shortstop Charlene Zwick brought Lewis home with a double of her own. Later, star batter Mica Morgan cleaned the bases with a grand slam that sent the ball sailing over the Edgewood Road fence.

Thanks to some fine fielding, the Mets were able to hold onto their lead. In the sixth inning, Valley Stream did manage to score a run, but the Mets rallied once more at the bottom of the inning and scored two of their own. The game ended shortly before dusk with a score of Mets 7, Valley Stream 5.

Stop and Record

How do the Mets win? What is the final score? Make notes on your 5 W's and H Organizer(page 70).

Nonfiction

C Plan

Now make a plan. How can you best uncover the facts of this news story?

• Use the strategy of summarizing when reading a news story.

During Reading

Now go back and read the news story on pages 68–69.

D Read with a Purpose

Use a 5 W's and H Organizer to help pull together key facts from the story.

Directions: Make notes on your 5 W's and H Organizer as you read.

5 W's and H Organizer

Who? the Mets vs. Valley Stream	What? a tough baseball game; the Mets win by a score of 7 to 5	When? yesterday afternoon (Saturday, May 10, 2003)

Subject: a baseball game

Where? the Mets' field	Why? The game is tough because Valley Stream is good.	How? The Mets win by scoring in the last innings of the game, after a pep talk from their coach.

These are the questions you should ask yourself while reading a newspaper article.

NAME

Using the Strategy

There are all kinds of tools you can use to keep track of facts and details in a news story. Choose the reading tools that work best for you.

• A Web is another way to keep track of key facts and details.

To make a Web, write the topic in the middle of the page. Then organize supporting information around the topic.

Directions: Complete this Web using facts from "Hamilton Mets Face Their Toughest Opponent to Date."

Web

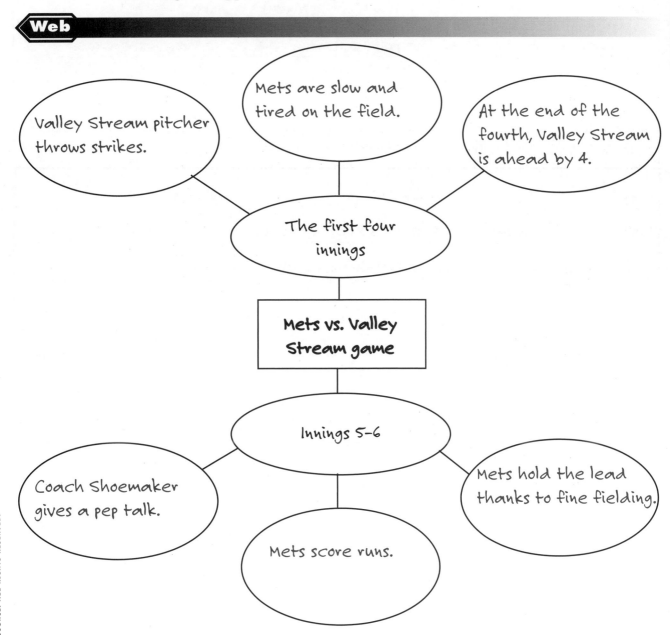

Understanding How News Stories Are Organized

In a news story, the lead gives the main ideas. The rest of the article *expands* on this information with details.

Directions: Take another look at the baseball article. What is the main idea? Which details support the main idea? Complete the organizer that follows. We've written some of the details for you.

Main Idea Organizer

Title: Hamilton Mets Face Their Toughest Opponent to Date

Main Idea: The Mets played the toughest game of the season yesterday in a home game against Valley Stream.

Detail 1	Detail 2	Detail 3
Valley Stream has a good pitcher who knows how to throw strikes.	The Mets had a tough time fielding against Valley Stream.	The Mets rallied in the second half to win the game.

Conclusion: It was a tough game, but the Mets are still undefeated.

E Connect

Making a connection to a newspaper article means reacting to what the reporter says.

• Record how the newspaper article made you feel.

<u>Directions:</u> Write your reaction to the Mets vs. Valley Stream article on the lines below.

The story about the Mets vs. Valley Stream baseball game made me feel excited because I was really eager to learn who won the game. Here's what it reminded me of in my own life: Sample answer: I played a really tough soccer game against kids in the next township. We had a hard time in the first half of the game, but then we scored some goals in the second.

After Reading

After you finish reading, think about the facts you've uncovered.

F Pause and Reflect

At this point, consider whether you've met your reading purpose.

• Ask yourself some questions about the news story you just read.

<u>Directions:</u> Complete this reading checklist.

Checklist	Yes	No
Do I know the subject of the story?	✔	
Do I know the main facts?	✔	
Can I answer who, what, where, when, why, and how?		✔

G Reread

If you're not quite clear on some of the facts of the story, it's a good idea to do some rereading.

• Use the strategy of reading critically to help you reread.

Reading critically means looking beyond the facts and details presented. It is reading "between the lines" to evaluate what the reporter wrote.

Directions: Reread parts of the baseball article. Then make notes on this Critical Reading Chart.

Critical Reading Chart

These are the kinds of questions you should ask yourself when you read critically.

Questions	My Evaluation
1. Is the main idea or viewpoint clear?	Yes, the main idea is clear. I understand that this was a really tough game.
2. Is there plenty of evidence to support the main idea?	Yes. The article tells all about the game.
3. Do the sources seem trustworthy?	The article would have been more trustworthy if it had given comments from players and fans.
4. Could there be another side to this story?	I'd like to know what the Valley Stream players had to say about the game.

Remember

Try to remember what you've read. You never know when the information will come in handy.

- **Writing an email about the news story can help you remember it.**

Directions: Write an email about the Mets vs. Valley Stream game to a friend or relative. Include the most important facts and details.

Email

Hi Aunt Louise!

Yesterday afternoon, the Mets scored a great win against the Valley Stream team. It was a very tough game. The Mets really messed up the first four innings. They couldn't score a run against the Valley Stream pitcher, and they were too tired to field well when Valley Stream was up to bat. Then the Mets coach talked to the team. He told them to pull themselves together and start working as a team. This really worked! In the last two innings of the game, the Mets really rallied. They scored a bunch of runs. They did some good fielding work and managed to keep most of the Valley Stream players off base. The final score was Mets 7, Valley Stream 5. Great game! :)

Chase

Focus on Personal Essays

Personal essays can be funny or serious. They can be sad or spooky. Your job as a reader is to understand the essay's subject and figure out what the author is trying to say about it.

Step 1: Find the subject and author's purpose.

The subject of an essay is *who* or *what* the author is talking about. The author's purpose may be to inform, persuade, or entertain.

Directions: Preview "Lesson Learned." Read the title and the first and last paragraphs. Skim the text. Look for the subject of the essay and the author's purpose. Then complete the sticky notes.

Lesson Learned

I'll never forget my first day at Eleanor Roosevelt Elementary. My family had just moved here from California. My mom signed me up for school right away, even though I told her there wasn't any rush. See, this would be my first time as "the new kid," and I wasn't very happy about it. I had seen new kids in my old school, and they all looked pretty miserable. But my mom signed me up anyway. She said I wouldn't be the new kid for long. As if that would make me feel better.

So on that first day of school, I felt really awful. I think I looked pretty miserable, too. Everyone stared when the principal walked me to my classroom. I saw dozens of pairs of eyes looking at my hair, my clothes, my shoes—even my backpack. I tried to stare back, but I didn't have the nerve. So basically I just got all red in the face and looked down at the floor.

After what seemed like an hour of staring, my new teacher showed me to my desk. Then she pretty much ignored me, and so did everyone else. This gave me a chance to look around, and I didn't like what I saw. No one in this classroom looked the least bit friendly. In fact, they all looked sort of mean and nasty. I could tell that they didn't want to have anything to do with me. I sort of felt like crying, but I didn't because it would have been

"Lesson Learned," continued

too embarrassing. So I closed my eyes real tight and just sat there.

At recess time, no one paid any attention to me, even though they needed an extra guy to play kickball. I could see what the kids were thinking: "Why bother with him? He's the new kid." So I just sat on a wall and watched a bunch of guys play kickball. At one point a kid looked over at me like he wanted to ask me to play, but I looked away. It wasn't worth the risk.

Actually, the second half of the day was a little better than the first. The teacher asked me to tell the class about California. Everyone looked really interested, and a couple of people asked me questions. They weren't mean and nasty questions, either. Later, the kid I saw on the kickball field took a seat by me in math. He asked me what it felt like to be the new kid. I told him it felt pretty awful—as awful as it gets. He didn't say anything after that, but he waited for me after school and we walked home together. It turns out he lives down my street a little ways.

When I got home from school, my mom asked me what I learned. She always asks that. I told her I learned what it was like to be the new kid. That made her look all serious and a tiny bit sad. But then I told her that the kids in the school seemed OK and that I might have made a friend. Right away, she was glad again.

What I didn't tell my mom was that I learned something else that day at school. Here's what I learned, and it's a pretty good lesson: No matter how hard it is, or how weird it feels, or how embarrassing or risky it seems, be nice to the new kid. Better yet, make friends with the new kid. The new kid will sure appreciate it. Trust me on this. I speak from experience.

I found these repeated words: I, school, kids, me

I think the subject of the essay is: being the new kid at school.

I think the author's purpose is: to persuade.

Nonfiction

Step 2: Find the main idea.

The main idea in a personal essay is what the author has to say about the subject. Use a formula like this one to find the main idea:

Finding the Main Idea

subject   +   what the author says about the subject   =   the main idea

School bus ride + It can be scary = A school bus ride can be a scary experience.

Directions: Complete this formula to find the main idea in "Lesson Learned."

Being the new kid   + It can be pretty awful.

(subject)   (what the author says about it)

= Being the new kid can be pretty awful.

(the main idea)

Step 3: Organize your thoughts.

Create an organizer that can help you remember the essay's main idea.

Directions: Complete this Main Idea Organizer. First write the main idea. Then write three details from the essay that support that idea.

Main Idea Organizer

Main Idea Being the new kid at school can be pretty awful.		
Detail 1	**Detail 2**	**Detail 3**
Kids stare at you.	They ignore you.	They forget to invite you to play.

Step 4: Evaluate the main idea.

Finish by thinking about how you feel about the essay. Do you agree or disagree with the author's main point? Have you had a similar experience or idea?

Directions: Write a journal entry about "Lesson Learned." Answer the questions above.

Journal Entry

I agree with the author's main point. I've never been a new kid myself, but I may be one in the future. I sure wouldn't like it if people stared at me. So I'm going to be really nice to the next new kid who comes to our classroom.

Nonfiction

Focus on Persuasive Writing

In persuasive writing, a writer gives an opinion or argues for a certain idea. Your job is to understand and evaluate the argument. This three-step plan can help.

Step 1: Find the topic and viewpoint.

First, figure out the **topic** of the writing. Then decide what the author's **viewpoint,** or opinion, is on the topic.

Directions: Read this editorial. Circle the topic. Highlight the author's viewpoint.

A Word about Grandparents

When I was little, I spent a lot of time at my Grandma Ruth's house. I'd go almost every day. We would bake bread or work in her garden or just sit on her porch. It was a quiet place, and I liked that.

But when I got older, I started seeing Grandma Ruth's house in a new light. A trip there took a lot of time. I was very busy. Plus, Grandma Ruth and I had nothing really in common, I argued. After all, she was eighty and I was twelve. What would we talk about?

So I stopped going to Grandma Ruth's house as often. I know she noticed, but she never said anything to me. She was always just the same whenever I did visit—warm and inviting and uncomplaining.

When I was fourteen, Grandma Ruth had to go into a nursing home in another state. We drove her there, and my aunt met us on the other end. I felt really bad then. I knew it would be a long time before I could visit my grandma again.

Does this story sound familiar to you? If it does, you're probably making the same mistake that I made. You've forgotten how important it is to appreciate your grandparents. It happens all the time.

"A Word about Grandparents," continued

But I'm telling you this is a mistake. Take the time now to appreciate your grandparents. It's foolish to be too busy to visit. If you wait too long, you may be too late. Grandparents have a lot to offer. They often have more time to listen and talk than your parents do. Plus, they have all those years of experience. Go for a visit, send a card, or pick up the phone. Do it today, rather than later. You'll be glad you did.

Step 2: Find support for the viewpoint.

Good persuasive writers give facts, examples, and reasons to support their viewpoint.

Directions: Read the editorial again. Underline three facts or reasons that the writer gives to support the argument.

Step 3: Evaluate the argument.

After reading, decide whether the writer persuaded you.

Directions: Complete this Critical Reading Chart. Write the author's viewpoint and support. Then give your own opinion.

Critical Reading Chart

1. Is the viewpoint clear? Yes. The author is saying to take the time now to appreciate your grandparents.

2. What evidence is presented? She uses her personal experience with her grandmother. She also says that grandparents have a lot to offer. They have more time to talk and years of experience.

3. Is it convincing? I think it makes a lot of sense. I like being with my grandfather. I hope I never get too busy to talk with him.

Focus on Biography

A biography tells an interesting story about a real person's life. It also paints a "portrait" of that person.

Step 1: Read for key events.

Directions: Read this excerpt from a biography about Cassius Clay, who is known to the world as Muhammad Ali. Underline three or four key events in Ali's life. Record them on the organizer.

> ### from *The Greatest: Muhammad Ali* by Walter Dean Myers

In 1954, twelve-year-old Cassius [Clay] rode his red-and-white Schwinn bicycle to the Columbia Auditorium in Louisville. He and a friend visited The Louisville Home Show, which was a predominantly black trade show. There was free candy and popcorn, and a general air of excitement as local merchants displayed their goods. When it was time to go, Cassius found that his bicycle was missing.

The Schwinn company made the most popular bicycles in the country, and Clay was angry and hurt that his had been stolen. The chance of his family scraping together the money for a new bicycle was slight, and Cassius was so upset that he was crying.

He wanted to report the bicycle stolen and was told that there was a policeman in the basement. Cassius found the officer, Joe Martin, and told him what had happened. He also added that when he found whoever had stolen his bike, he was going to beat him up.

Joe Martin had been a member of the Louisville police force for years. He enjoyed working with young people, black and white, and taught boxing at the Columbia Gym.

"You thinking about beating somebody up, you had better learn to fight," he told the eighty-nine-pound Cassius. That suited the boy. He wanted to teach the bike thief a lesson and in his twelve-year-old mind he could imagine himself beating up the perpetrator. Cassius started boxing lessons.

Story String

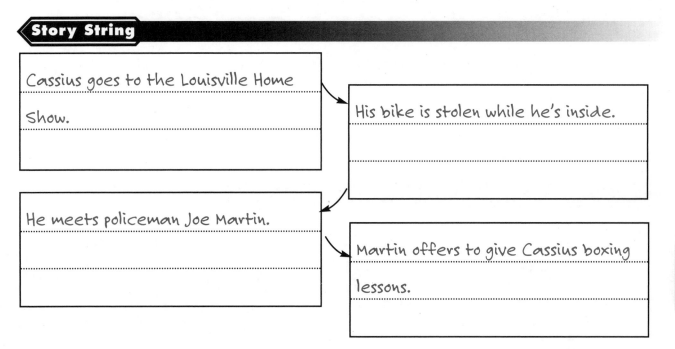

Cassius goes to the Louisville Home Show.

His bike is stolen while he's inside.

He meets policeman Joe Martin.

Martin offers to give Cassius boxing lessons.

Step 2: Form a portrait of the subject.

As you read, look for clues about the subject's personality. When you do this, you are forming your own portrait, or picture, of the subject.

Directions: Complete this Thinking Tree about Cassius Clay. Write words that describe Clay. Then note the details that support the words you've chosen. We've chosen one descriptive word for you.

Thinking Tree

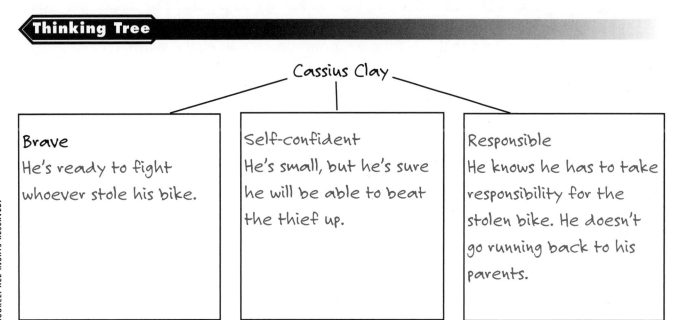

Cassius Clay

Brave
He's ready to fight whoever stole his bike.

Self-confident
He's small, but he's sure he will be able to beat the thief up.

Responsible
He knows he has to take responsibility for the stolen bike. He doesn't go running back to his parents.

Step 3: Discover cause and effect.

Next, put the facts together to figure out *why* the subject believed in certain things or made important decisions.

Directions: Complete this Cause-Effect Organizer about Cassius Clay. Use your own knowledge plus what you've learned from the biography.

Cause-Effect Organizer

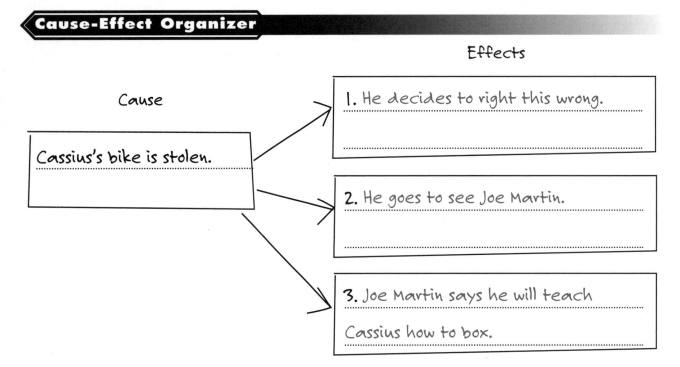

Effects

Cause

Cassius's bike is stolen.

1. He decides to right this wrong.

2. He goes to see Joe Martin.

3. Joe Martin says he will teach Cassius how to box.

Step 4: Respond to the biographical subject.

It's important that you form your own impression of the subject. Your opinion may or may not be the same as the biographer's opinion.

Directions: Write your opinion of Cassius Clay. Then explain why you feel that way.

Opinion Statement

I really admire Muhammad Ali. He has overcome so much in his life. I'd never heard this story about the bike. I think it shows a lot about Ali's character. He's determined.

Focus on Real-world Writing

Real-world writing keeps you informed. Here's a plan to find and remember the information you need.

Step 1: Know what you're after.

First, figure out your reading purpose. Ask yourself, "What do I need to know?"

Directions: Look at this notice about an upcoming assembly. Suppose this was an assembly at your school. Write your purpose for reading the notice.

My purpose: I need to find out what will happen at the assembly and where and when it will take place.

ASSEMBLY! ASSEMBLY! ASSEMBLY! ASSEMBLY!

This Friday will be our annual Meet-the-Author Assembly in the Elmwood Elementary Auditorium.

All students are required to attend.

Date: Friday, December 1

Time: 9:15 AM sharp

Author: Joy Eileen Hopkins, author of the *Swamp River School* series

Sponsor: Elmwood PTO

Here is your chance to meet a world-famous author. Ms. Hopkins will discuss her fabulous book series and her plans for future books. At the end of the assembly, she will take questions from the audience. Come prepared with at least one question for the author.

Copies of Ms. Hopkins's books will be on sale in the cafeteria for $12.95 each. Proceeds will benefit the Elmwood PTO.

Step 2: Figure out how the material is organized.

To understand how real-world reading material is organized, look for these features in your preview.

Preview Checklist

☑ main headings and titles

☑ boldfaced and emphasized words

☑ lists or outlines

Directions: Preview the flyer. Write what you noticed on the lines below.

The title tells me: there will be an assembly.

The boldfaced words make it easy to find: the date, time, speaker, and sponsor.

Some other important information is: how to buy the author's books.

Step 3: Skim for what you need to know.

Not all information in real-world writing is equally important. Pay attention to what *you personally* need to know.

NAME _____

Directions: Look at the Web below. Skim the notice to find information to complete this Web.

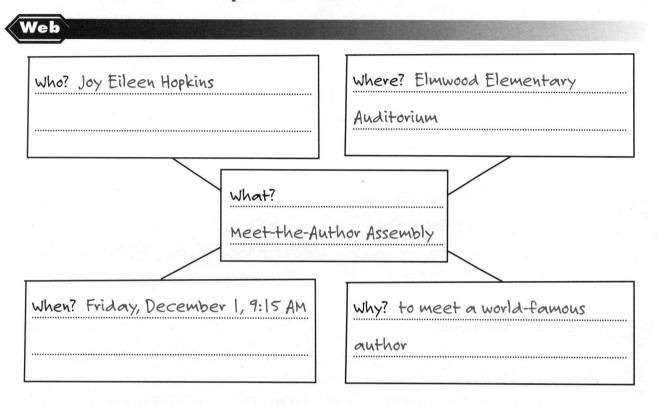

Web

Who? Joy Eileen Hopkins

Where? Elmwood Elementary Auditorium

What?
Meet-the-Author Assembly

When? Friday, December 1, 9:15 AM

Why? to meet a world-famous author

Step 4: Remember and use the information.

Taking notes is a good way to remember key information.

Directions: Write information about the assembly on this calendar page. Include the most important details.

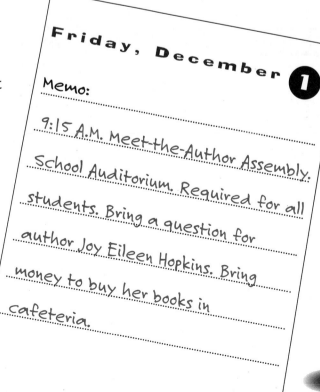

Friday, December 1

Memo:

9:15 A.M. Meet-the-Author Assembly.
School Auditorium. Required for all
students. Bring a question for
author Joy Eileen Hopkins. Bring
money to buy her books in
cafeteria.

Reading a Folktale

Folktales are stories that usually contain a lesson. They are often fun to read, with amusing characters and surprise endings. As you read a folktale, also think about what the lesson means to you.

Before Reading

Let the reading process and the strategy of using graphic organizers help you read a folktale.

A Set a Purpose

Since most folktales tell a lesson, you can use that as your purpose for reading.

• **To set your purpose, ask one question about the plot of the folktale and another question about the lesson it teaches.**

Directions: Write your purpose for the Yoruban folktale "How Tortoise Grew a Tail" here. Then make a prediction about the story.

Purpose question #1 *What is "How Tortoise Grew a Tail" about? or What happens in the story?*

Purpose question #2 *What lesson will I learn from this story? or How does that lesson apply to me?*

My prediction: *I think this story will have a tortoise as its main character. I predict that he grows a tail because someone asks him to or makes him do it.*

NAME ....

B Preview

Next, preview the folktale that follows. Read the title. Skim the folktale for repeated words or names. Read the first and last paragraphs.

Directions: Write your notes in this chart.

Preview Chart

Preview Questions	My Notes
What is the title of the tale?	"How Tortoise Grew a Tail"
Where does the story come from?	It comes from the Yoruban people of West Africa.
What repeated words and names did you see?	tortoise, boa, Ijapa, Ojola, so, vegetables, bowl, tail
What did you learn from the first paragraph?	The tortoise's name is Ijapa. He has been traveling. He goes to his friend Ojola's house. Ojola is a boa.
What did you learn from the last paragraph?	Our friends can teach us to be both short and tall.

Fiction

HOW **TORTOISE GREW A TAIL**

A YORUBAN FOLKTALE FROM WEST AFRICA

Ijapa the tortoise had traveled for days under the hot, bright sun. Because of all this walking, he was hot, tired, and very hungry. Eventually, he arrived at the house of his friend, Ojola, the boa. Ijapa went to the door and called to Ojola, asking for something to eat. When Ojola saw how hot and tired Ijapa was, he invited him in. He said:

"Come in, Ijapa, and rest yourself. You are hot and tired. Please sit down and make yourself at home."

So Ijapa came in Ojola's house and they sat down together to talk. The whole time they talked, Ojola's wife was cooking, and Ijapa could smell the wonderful smells coming from the pot. He began to groan and cry from hunger. The boa asked:

"Does the smell of the cooking bother you?"

"No," replied Ijapa, "it just reminds me of home, where I would be eating a lovely supper cooked by my devoted wife."

"Well, tonight you shall eat with us," said Ojola. "Go wash yourself and all will be ready."

So Ijapa went out back on his tired feet and walked to the stream. He washed as quickly as he could. Feeling refreshed, he walked back to the boa's house. Upon entering, he saw a large bowl full of steaming hot vegetables and corn sitting on the floor in the center of the room.

Stop and Record

Make some notes in the "Beginning" section of the Story Organizer on page 93.

"Mmmm!" said Ijapa, licking his lips. "Those vegetables smell just right!"

"Just come here and help yourself," said Ojola as he wrapped himself around the bowl and began to eat.

"How Tortoise Grew a Tail," continued

When Ijapa saw the boa's thick coils wrapped around the bowl, he began walking around to see if he could find a spot near the bowl. But on all sides Ojola's fat coils were piled up around the bowl. All the while, Ojola slurped and supped and supped and slurped. Then he said:

"Ijapa, this is just delicious. What are you waiting for? Do join me before it's all gone."

"Yes, I would like to join you," replied Ijapa. "But Ojola, you've wrapped yourself around the food and I can't get near it."

"Ijapa, this is our custom," the boa replied smoothly. "We always eat our food this way. So come and eat before it is gone and my offer means nothing."

So the poor tortoise scuttled this way and that, back and forth, but still couldn't find a way in. Finally, the boa swallowed the last mouthful and sighed.

"Well, it is nice to eat with friends," said Ojola. "We must do this again."

Ijapa said nothing. He did not complain. He bade farewell to Ojola and began walking home. But his mood was very bad, and he was still so very hungry. When he got home, he thought about how he could teach Ojola a lesson. He decided to invite him to his own house for the next festival day to return his hospitality.

Stop and Record

Make some notes in the "Middle" section of the Story Organizer on page 93.

On the next festival day, Ijapa's wife prepared a fine meal. Ijapa spent the day weaving a long, fat tail out of grass. When it was finished, he stuck it on himself with tree gum.

When Ojola arrived, the tortoise greeted him at the door and invited him in. He said:

"Come in, friend Ojola, and make yourself comfortable."

So the boa came in and the two friends sat down to talk. Ojola could smell the wonderful aroma coming from the cooking pot. He licked his lips and said:

"That cooking smells good, Ijapa. What are we going to eat?"

"You'll soon see, Ojola," said the tortoise. "You go and wash and all will be ready."

Fiction

"How Tortoise Grew a Tail," continued

So Ojola went to the spring in back to wash. Feeling refreshed, he came back inside to find that a big feast was laid out in the middle of the floor.

"Mmmm!" said Ojola, licking his lips. "Those vegetables smell just right!"

"Just come here and help yourself," said Ijapa as he circled round and round his food until his fat tail made of grass surrounded the pot on all sides. Then the tortoise began to eat.

Ojola, seeing the tortoise's strange new tail wrapped around the food, slithered around to the other side to find a way in. But Ijapa's tail was piled up around the food. All the while, Ijapa slurped and supped and supped and slurped. Then he said:

"Ojola, this is just delicious. What are you waiting for? Do join me before it's all gone."

"Yes, I would like to join you," replied Ojola. "But tell me, where did you get this big new tail? Before you were short, but now you are very long, and your tail is in my way."

"One learns about such things from one's friends," replied the tortoise.

So Ojola remembered how when Ijapa was his guest, he had wrapped his coils around the food and prevented his friend from eating. Ojola was ashamed. Without saying another word, he went home.

From this event comes the proverb:

We learn from our friends to be short
And we also learn to be tall.

Stop and Record
Make some notes in the "End" section of the Story Organizer on page 93.

C Plan

Next make a plan. Choose a strategy that can help you understand the folktale and the lesson it teaches.

- **The strategy of using graphic organizers works well with folktales.**

NAME

During Reading

Now go back and do a careful reading of the folktale.

D Read with a Purpose

A Story Organizer like the one below can help you keep track of key events in the folktale. It simplifies the tale and makes it easier to see what happens.

Directions: As you read, make notes on this Story Organizer.

Story Organizer

Beginning	Middle	End
What happens?	What happens?	What happens?
A turtle who is hot and tired arrives at his friend's house. His friend, a boa, invites him to stay for dinner.	The turtle can't eat because the boa is curled around the bowl. The boa eats all the food, and the turtle goes home hungry and angry. He decides to teach his friend a lesson.	The turtle invites his friend for dinner. He wraps his grass tail around the bowl of food so that the boa can't get anything to eat. The boa realizes what he has done to his friend, and he goes home ashamed.

Fiction

Using the Strategy

All kinds of graphic organizers work with folktales. Choose the one that works best for you.

• **A Story String helps you keep track of what happens event by event.**

Directions: Tell what happens in "How Tortoise Grew a Tail" on this Story String.

Story String

1. Ijapa arrives at the home of Ojola. Ojola invites Ijapa to eat.

2. Ijapa goes to wash. When he returns, he sees the food.

3. Ojola wraps his tail around the food so that Ijapa can't get any.

4. Ijapa goes home hungry and angry and makes a plan.

5. Ijapa makes a grass tail and invites Ojola to eat.

6. Ijapa plays the same trick on Ojola.

7. Ojola is ashamed for hurting his friend.

94

Understanding How Folktales Are Organized

All folktales are different, of course. But most follow a similar pattern.

Directions: Reread page 220 in your handbook. Then complete this Plot Diagram for "How Tortoise Grew a Tail."

Plot Diagram

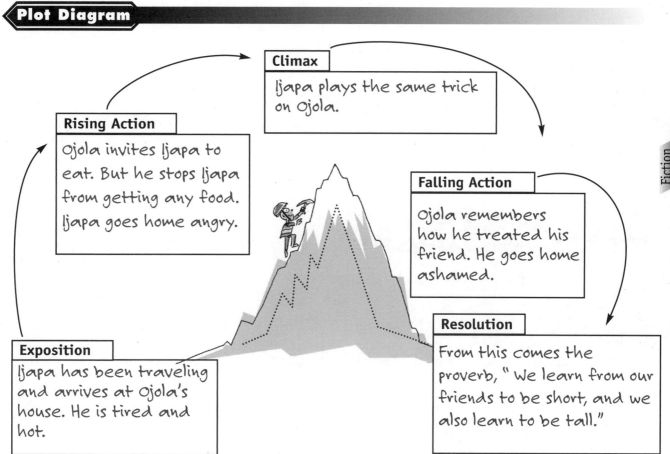

Climax

Ijapa plays the same trick on Ojola.

Rising Action

Ojola invites Ijapa to eat. But he stops Ijapa from getting any food. Ijapa goes home angry.

Falling Action

Ojola remembers how he treated his friend. He goes home ashamed.

Exposition

Ijapa has been traveling and arrives at Ojola's house. He is tired and hot.

Resolution

From this comes the proverb, "We learn from our friends to be short, and we also learn to be tall."

Fiction

E Connect

As you read, try to make connections to the folktale. How do you feel about the characters? Has something like this ever happened to you?

• **Making connections to a folktale can help you understand its lesson.**

Directions: Explain your connections to the characters in the folktale you just read.

This is how I feel about the boa: I think he is really mean.

because he invited Ijapa to eat and then wouldn't share any food.

This is how I feel about the tortoise: I felt sorry for him when he was at Ojola's house.

Then I started to admire him

because he found a way to teach the boa a lesson.

After Reading

After you finish a tale, pull together what you've learned.

F Pause and Reflect

Think again about the two purpose questions you wrote before reading.

- **Ask yourself, "Do I know what the folktale is about? Do I understand the lesson to be learned?"**

Directions: Circle the answers that apply to you. Then explain.

(I know what the folktale is about.)   I don't know what the folktale is about.

I understand the folktale's lesson.   (I don't understand the folktale's lesson.)

Here's why: I understand what happens in the story, but I'm not really sure what

the lesson is. Also, I'm not sure what the proverb at the end means.

Reread

If you still have questions, reread key parts of the folktale.

• **Use the rereading strategy of close reading.**

Directions: Look at these lines from the folktale. Write your thoughts and feelings about each.

Double-entry Journal

Text	What I Think about It
"Ijapa, this is our custom," the boa replied smoothly. "We always eat our food this way."	Is this really his custom? He's making it impossible for Ijapa to eat. It's really mean of him.
"One learns about such things from one's friends," replied the tortoise.	The tortoise is teaching the boa a lesson about being a friend. I'm glad that Ijapa did this. Ojola got what he deserved.
We learn from our friends to be short And we also learn to be tall.	I think this means that we can learn both bad things and good things from our friends. It's up to us to decide how to use what we learn.

 Remember

Good readers remember what they've read.

• **Make a folktale your own by "translating" it into the modern day.**

Directions: Turn "How Tortoise Got a Tail" into a modern-day story. Write the first part of the story on the lines below.

Story Opener

Last week, my friend Katya invited me over for a sleepover. She said that she

would give me the best spot in her bed and the nicest breakfast I had ever

had. I thought this sounded great, so I said "yes" to her offer.

Reading a Novel

The author of a novel creates a whole world for you to explore. There are characters to meet, settings to imagine, and action to get caught up in. Practice using the reading process with a novel here.

Before Reading

In a novel, there's so much going on! How can you figure out what's really important? Use the reading process and the strategy of synthesizing to help.

A Set a Purpose

Your first purpose when reading a novel is to enjoy it. But you also need to understand what you're reading.

- **To set your purpose, ask important questions about the characters, setting, plot, and theme.**

Directions: You will be reading part of a famous novel called *The Wind in the Willows*. What should be your purpose for reading? Write some questions below. (We've done the first one for you.)

Purpose Chart

Element	My Questions
characters	Who are the most important characters?
setting	Where and when does the story take place?
plot	What happens in this novel? or What is the action all about?
theme	What is the theme of this novel? or What are the big ideas?

B Preview

Preview a novel before you read it. Begin by looking at the front and back covers. What can you learn about the book and the author?

Directions: Preview the front and back covers of *The Wind in the Willows.* Complete the sticky notes.

Back Cover

Meet some new friends in Kenneth Grahame's amazing *The Wind in the Willows* . . .

THE WIND IN THE WILLOWS is the story of Mole, Rat, Badger, and Toad—four good friends who roam the river banks in search of fun and adventure. In their travels, the four friends learn about loyalty, kindness, and courage.

The Wind in the Willows began as a series of bedtime stories that Kenneth Grahame made up for his four-year-old son. Grahame's son quickly grew to love his father's stories and told him he should write them down for all children to enjoy. Wisely, Grahame listened to his son and gave the world *The Wind in the Willows*, one of the most well-loved novels of all time.

Front Cover

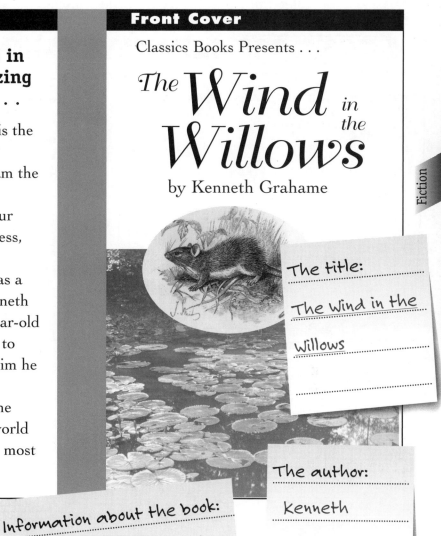

Classics Books Presents . . .

The Wind *in the* Willows

by Kenneth Grahame

Fiction

The title:

The Wind in the

Willows

The author:

Kenneth

Grahame

Information about the author:

Kenneth Grahame wrote

the novel after telling the

story to his son at bedtime.

Information about the book:

It is about Mole, Rat, Badger,

and Toad. They have

adventures along a river

bank. They learn about

loyalty, kindness, and

courage.

C Plan

Good readers use the strategy of synthesizing when reading a novel.

• **Synthesizing means pulling together all the elements of the novel—character, setting, plot, and theme.**

Directions: Make notes on this Fiction Organizer as you read the selection from *The Wind in the Willows*.

Fiction Organizer

Characters Who are they? What are they like?

Mole: cautious and polite; honest

Rat: creative and fun-loving;

cheerful; good-natured

Setting Where and when does the story take place?

near a river bank on a bright summer

morning

Title
The Wind in the Willows

Plot What happens?

Rat sits by the side of the river and teases the ducks. Mole invites Rat to call on Mr. Toad. They both jump in their boat and sail down the river toward Toad Hall.

Theme What "big ideas" might the novel be about? friendship, adventure, having fun

NAME ....

During Reading

D Read with a Purpose

Now read this part of *The Wind in the Willows*.

Directions: As you read, make notes on your Fiction Organizer.

> from *The Wind in the Willows* by Kenneth Grahame

Chapter II
THE OPEN ROAD

"RATTY," said the Mole suddenly, one bright summer morning, "if you please, I want to ask you a favour."

The Rat was sitting on the river bank, singing a little song. He had just composed it himself, so he was very taken up with it, and would not pay proper attention to Mole or anything else. Since early morning he had been swimming in the river, in company with his friends the ducks. And when the ducks stood on their heads suddenly, as ducks will, he would dive down and tickle their necks, just under where their chins would be if ducks had chins, till they were forced to come to the surface again in a hurry, spluttering and angry and shaking their feathers at him, for it is impossible to say quite *all* you feel when your head is under water.

Stop and Record
Make some notes in the "Setting" section of the Fiction Organizer on page 100.

At last they implored him to go away and attend to his own affairs and leave them to mind theirs. So the Rat went away, and sat on the river bank in the sun, and made up a song about them, which he called

"DUCKS' DITTY"
All along the backwater,
Through the rushes tall,
Ducks are a-dabbling,
Up tails all!

Fiction

from *The Wind in the Willows* by Kenneth Grahame, continued

Ducks' tails, drakes' tails,
Yellow feet a-quiver,
Yellow bills all out of sight
Busy in the river!

Slushy green undergrowth
Where the roach swim—
Here we keep our larder,
Cool and full and dim.

Everyone for what he likes!
We like to be
Heads down, tails up,
Dabbling free!

High in the blue above
Swifts whirl and call—
We are down a-dabbling
Up tails all!

"I don't know that I think so *very* much of that little song, Rat,"
observed the Mole cautiously. He was no poet himself and didn't care who
knew it; and he had a candid nature.

Stop and Record

*Make some notes about Mole in the "Character" section of the
Fiction Organizer on page 100.*

"Nor don't the ducks neither," replied the Rat cheerfully. "They say,
'*Why* can't fellows be allowed to do what they like *when* they like and *as*
they like, instead of other fellows sitting on banks and watching them all
the time and making remarks and poetry and things about them? What
nonsense it all is!' That's what the ducks say."
"So it is, so it is," said the Mole, with great heartiness.
"No, it isn't!" cried the Rat indignantly.

from *The Wind In the Willows* by Kenneth Grahame, continued

"Well then, it isn't, it isn't," replied the Mole soothingly. "But what I wanted to ask you was, won't you take me to call on Mr. Toad? I've heard so much about him, and I do so want to make his acquaintance."

"Why, certainly," said the good-natured Rat, jumping to his feet and dismissing poetry from his mind for the day. "Get the boat out, and we'll paddle up there at once. It's never the wrong time to call on Toad. Early or late he's always the same fellow. Always good-tempered, always glad to see you, always sorry when you go!"

Stop and Record

Make some notes about Rat in the "Character" section of the Fiction Organizer on page 100.

"He must be a very nice animal," observed the Mole, as he got into the boat and took the sculls, while the Rat settled himself comfortably in the stern.

"He is indeed the best of animals," replied Rat. "So simple, so good-natured, and so affectionate. Perhaps he's not very clever—we can't all be geniuses; and it may be that he is both boastful and conceited. But he has got some great qualities, has Toady."

Rounding a bend in the river, they came in sight of a handsome, dignified old house of mellowed red brick, with well-kept lawns reaching down to the water's edge.

"There's Toad Hall," said the Rat; "and that creek on the left, where the notice-board says, 'Private. No landing allowed,' leads to his boat-house, where we'll leave the boat. The stables are over there to the right. That's the banqueting-hall you're looking at now—very old, that is. Toad is rather rich, you know, and this is really one of the nicest houses in these parts, though we never admit as much to Toad."

Stop and Record

Make some notes in the "Plot" and "Theme" sections of the Fiction Organizer on page 100.

Fiction

Using the Strategy

Synthesizing can help you pull together everything you learn about a character to understand that character.

- **Use the strategy of synthesizing to help you understand a novel's characters.**

Directions: Write notes about Rat on the Character Map below.

Character Map

What He Says and Does

- swims in the river
- tickles the ducks underwater
- makes up a silly song
- agrees to go visit Mr. Toad
- tells Mole a lot about Mr. Toad

What Others Think about Him

Mole is a little cautious with him, as if he's worried about getting Rat upset.

RAT

How He Looks and Feels

- feels cheerful and happy

How I Feel about Him

Sample response: I think he's funny.

Only someone funny would think to tickle ducks under their necks.

Understanding How Novels Are Organized

The plot of a novel is just as important as the characters. Usually, the events of a plot follow chronological, or time, order.

• **You can use a Story String to show the sequence of events in a plot.**

Directions: Use this Story String to show what happens in this part of *The Wind in the Willows.*

◄ **Story String** ▶

1. Rat teases the ducks in the river.

2. He makes up a song and sings it to Mole.

3. Mole says he doesn't really care for the song, and the two argue about ducks for a while.

4. Mole asks Rat to take him to meet Mr. Toad.

5. The two animals jump in their boat and paddle off.

6. They arrive at Toad Hall.

Fiction

E Connect

As you read, ask yourself, "How do I feel about the characters and plot?" This question can help you feel involved in what you're reading.

• **Good readers make connections between the novel and their own lives.**

Directions: Here is a Double-entry Journal. Read the quotes from the novel in the left-hand column. Tell how they make you feel in the right-hand column.

Double-entry Journal

Quotes	My Thoughts
"I don't know that I think so very much of that little song, Rat," observed the Mole cautiously.	Mole speaks his mind, but he does it carefully. He doesn't want to hurt Rat's feelings.
"Perhaps he's not very clever—we can't all be geniuses; and it may be that he is both boastful and conceited."	These are negative comments about Mr. Toad. I wonder why Rat and Mole want to visit him.
"Toad is rather rich, you know, and this is really one of the nicest houses in these parts, though we never admit as much to Toad."	They won't tell Toad this because it will make him even more boastful. I think Rat and Mole might envy Toad a little.

After Reading

After you finish a novel, take a few minutes to think about some of its "big ideas." Pull all of its parts together—the characters, setting, plot, and theme.

F Pause and Reflect

Think back on what you've read.

• Ask yourself, "How well did I meet my purpose?"

Directions: Put a √ in the column that tells how well you understand the elements in this novel.

Checklist

Element	I understand it very well.	I need to understand it better.
characters	✔	
setting		✔
plot	✔	
theme		✔

G Reread

If you're not sure how an element works in a novel, you may need to do some rereading.

• Use a graphic organizer to keep track of what you learn.

Directions: Return to the reading from *The Wind in the Willows*. Look for clues about the setting. Write what you find here.

Setting Chart

Clues about Time	Clues about Place
Time of Day	Where does the action take place?
"one bright summer morning;" Rat is sitting in the sun.	Rat is sitting on the river bank; Rat and Mole paddle a boat down the river.
Season	What is this place like?
Summer. It's warm and sunny.	It is filled with wildlife. The river bank has docks for boats.

H Remember

If you're reading a novel for a class assignment, you will need to *remember* what you've read.

• **To remember a novel, take notes to summarize each chapter.**

Directions: Write a summary of this part of *The Wind in the Willows*.

Chapter-by-Chapter Summary Notes

Chapter 11

Rat makes up a silly song about ducks as he sits by the river. Mole asks Rat to take him to Toad Hall to meet Mr. Toad. Rat and Mole paddle a boat down the river to Toad Hall. Rat tells Mole that Mr. Toad is good-natured and kind, but not very smart. Mr. Toad is rich and lives in a big house.

Focus on Characters

Some characters are so real, you feel like they could jump right off the page. The more you get to know the characters in a text, the better you understand them. Follow these steps to focus on characters.

Step 1: Note what the character says and does.

Directions: Read this part of *Ramona's World*. Highlight everything Ramona *says*. Underline what she *does*.

from *Ramona's World* by Beverly Cleary

Mrs. Meacham explained. "Today we are going to study words we use. When we wrote about ourselves, we discovered words we need to learn how to spell."

Ramona looked more closely at the words on the chalkboard. Among them she saw *scream, hungry, couch, finger, role, model*. They looked familiar. They were familiar. They were her words. She scowled.

"Is something the matter, Ramona?" asked Mrs. Meacham, who had been quick to learn names.

Ramona decided to speak up. "What difference does spelling make if people know what you mean?" she asked.

"You wouldn't want people to think you sat on a coach instead of a couch, would you?" Mrs. Meacham asked.

The class found this funny, but Ramona did not, not when the class laughed. She felt her face grow hot. She slid down in her seat and shook her head. Mrs. Meacham knew the answer. Why did she bother to ask?

Mrs. Meacham continued, "And before lunch are you hungry or hungry?"

The class laughed, harder this time. The warm day suddenly seemed warmer. Ramona decided right then that she *did not like Mrs. Meacham*, and this was only the second day of school. Mrs. Meacham did not tell the truth. She said learning was fun, and it wasn't. At least not all the time. Not when it came to spelling.

Fiction

Step 2: Create a Character Map.

Use a Character Map to keep track of details about the character.

Directions: Complete this Character Map about Ramona.

Character Map

What the Character Says	What the Character Does
She tells her teacher that correct spelling isn't important.	She scowls. She slides down in her seat.

Ramona

How the Character Feels	What Others Think About the Character
She is angry at her teacher. She is upset when the other kids laugh.	Mrs. Meacham seems hard on Ramona. Maybe she doesn't like her.

Step 3: Make inferences about the character.

Finish by making some reasonable guesses about the character.

Directions: Write your inferences about Ramona in the chart.

Inference Chart

What Character Does and Says	What I Conclude
"She scowled."	She is mad.
"She felt her face grow hot."	She is embarrassed.
"Ramona decided right then that she *did not like Mrs. Meacham*, and this was only the second day of school."	She gets mad easily.

Focus on  Setting

Setting is where and when a story happens. Very often, setting affects the characters and mood of a story. Follow these five steps to understand a setting.

Step 1: Find clues about the setting.

Directions: Read this excerpt from *The Story of Doctor Dolittle.* Highlight clues about time. Underline clues about place.

> ### from *The Story of Doctor Dolittle* by Hugh Lofting
>
> ONCE upon a time, many years ago when our grandfathers were little children—there was a doctor; and his name was Dolittle—John Dolittle, M.D. "M.D." means that he was a proper doctor and knew a whole lot.
>
> He lived in a little town called, Puddleby-on-the-Marsh. All the folks, young and old, knew him well by sight. And whenever he walked down the street in his high hat everyone would say, "There goes the Doctor!—He's a clever man." And the dogs and the children would all run up and follow behind him; and even the crows that lived in the church-tower would caw and nod their heads.
>
> The house he lived in, on the edge of the town, was quite small; but his garden was very large and had a wide lawn and stone seats and weeping-willows hanging over. His sister, Sarah Dolittle, was housekeeper for him; but the Doctor looked after the garden himself.
>
> He was very fond of animals and kept many kinds of pets. Besides the gold-fish in the pond at the bottom of his garden, he had rabbits in the pantry, white mice in his piano, a squirrel in the linen closet and a hedgehog in the cellar. He had a cow with a calf too, and an old lame horse—twenty-five years of age—and chickens, and pigeons, and two lambs, and many other animals. But his favorite pets were Dab-Dab the duck, Jip the dog, Gub-Gub the baby pig, Polynesia the parrot, and the owl Too-Too.

Fiction

Step 2: Organize important details.

Use a Setting Chart to keep track of the clues you find about time and place.

Directions: Complete this Setting Chart for *The Story of Doctor Dolittle*.

Setting Chart

Clues about Time	Clues about Place
Past, present, or future?	Place name:
Past—"Once upon a time, many years ago when our grand-fathers were little children"	a little town called Puddleby-on-the-Marsh
	What the house looks like:
Doctor Dolittle wears a "high hat."	It's a small house with a large garden. There are animals everywhere, inside and outside of the house.

Step 3: Picture the setting.

Drawing the scene will help you see the setting more clearly.

Directions: Make a sketch of Doctor Dolittle's house and garden.

Sketch of Setting

Step 4: Draw conclusions about the mood.

The setting can affect the mood, or general feeling, of a story. The mood of a story can be happy or sad, peaceful or tense, funny or scary.

Directions: Complete this Double-entry Journal. What do these details about the setting tell you about the mood of the story?

Double-entry Journal

Quotes	My Thoughts about the Mood
"Once upon a time, many years ago when our grandfathers were little children . . ."	This story has a fairy tale mood. It's set a long time ago, and you think maybe magical things will happen.
" . . . but his garden was very large and had a wide lawn and stone seats and weeping-willows hanging over."	The mood is inviting and relaxing. It sounds like a peaceful place.

Step 5: Draw conclusions about the characters.

The setting in a story can tell you a lot about the characters.

Directions: Complete this chart. Tell what the house is like. Then write what the setting tells you about Dr. Dolittle.

Inference Chart

Doctor Dolittle's House	What This Tells Me about Dr. Dolittle
The house is small, but the garden is large and filled with plants and trees. There are animals inside and outside the house.	He loves animals and nature.

Fiction

Focus on Dialogue

When you read dialogue, pay attention to who is speaking, what is being said, and how it is being said. Follow these steps.

Step 1: Do a close reading.

First, read the dialogue slowly and carefully. Make notes as you go.

Directions: Read this dialogue from a famous novel. Then answer questions about what you've read.

> **from *From the Mixed-Up Files of Mrs. Basil E. Frankweiler* by E. L. Konigsburg**

As soon as they reached the sidewalk, Jamie made his first decision as treasurer. "We'll walk from here to the museum."

"Walk?" Claudia asked. "Do you realize that it is over forty blocks from here?"

"Well, how much does the bus cost?"

"The bus!" Claudia exclaimed. "Who said anything about taking a bus? I want to take a taxi."

"Claudia," Jamie said, "you are quietly out of your mind. How can you even think of a taxi? We have no more allowance. No more income. You can't be extravagant any longer. It's not my money we're spending. It's *our* money. We're in this together, remember?"

"You're right," Claudia answered. "A taxi is expensive. The bus is cheaper. It's only twenty cents each. We'll take the bus."

"*Only* twenty cents each. That's forty

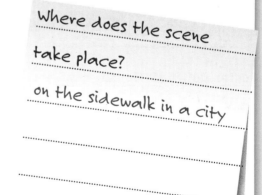

Who is talking?

Jamie and Claudia

Where does the scene take place?

on the sidewalk in a city

from *From the Mixed-Up Files of Mrs. Basil E. Frankweiler* by E. L. Konigsburg

cents total. No bus. We'll walk."

"We'll wear out forty cents worth of shoe leather, " Claudia mumbled. "You're sure we have to walk?"

"Positive," Jamie answered. "Which way do we go?"

"Sure you won't change your mind?" The look on Jamie's face gave her the answer. She sighed. No wonder Jamie had more than twenty-four dollars; he was a gambler and a cheapskate. If that's the way he wants to be, she thought, I'll never again ask him for bus fare; I'll suffer and never, never let him know about it. But he'll regret it when I simply collapse from exhaustion. I'll collapse quietly.

What are the characters talking about? how to get to the museum. Claudia wants to take a taxi or the bus. Jamie says no because it is too expensive.

How are they saying it? Jamie says things in a strong voice. Claudia asks more questions. She is not as sure about things.

Which character reminds you more of yourself?
Answers will vary.
Possible: Jamie

Why? Jamie is really smart, and I am too. He saves his money, and so do I.

Fiction

Step 2: Look for clues about character.

Think about what the dialogue shows you about each character.

Directions: Write your ideas about Claudia and Jamie here. Explain your evidence.

◀ **Inference Chart**

Character	Personality	Evidence from Dialogue
Claudia	She might be a little lazy. She doesn't know as many things as Jamie. She is not the type to give up easily.	She doesn't want to walk, so she asks to take a taxi, and then a bus. She does what Jamie says, but she's kind of upset about it.
Jamie	Jamie is smart. He speaks his mind. He thinks it's OK to boss Claudia around.	Jamie is the treasurer. You have to be smart for that job. He isn't worried that Claudia will get mad at him. He just says what he wants.

Step 3: Look for clues about plot.

Dialogue often gives you clues about the plot. The characters discuss what may happen next or what has happened in the past.

Directions: Predict what you think will happen next in the story you just read. Then explain your prediction.

My prediction: I think Claudia and Jamie will begin walking to the museum. But something might go wrong along the way, and Claudia could say, "I told you so."

Explanation: Jamie gets his way, but you can tell that Claudia is not happy about it.

Step 4: Look for clues about mood.

What the characters say and how they say it can affect a story's mood, or the feeling in the story.

Directions: Read the lines below. Tell what mood is created by each example of dialogue.

◄ **Double-entry Journal**

Dialogue	What Is the Mood?
"Walk?" Claudia asked. "Do you realize that it is over forty blocks from here?"	It's a little bit tense, like a fight between brother and sister.
"Claudia," Jamie said, "you are quietly out of your mind. How can you even think about a taxi?"	a little more tense, but still quiet
"You can't be extravagant any longer. It's not my money we're spending. It's our money. We're in this together, remember?"	Now the mood is not as tense. The argument is ending. Jamie is very sensible.

Focus on Plot

Plot is the actions or series of events in a work of fiction.
Follow these steps to understand a plot.

Step 1: Find the conflict.

Usually, the plot of a story involves a problem or conflict.

Directions: Read this fairy tale. Watch for the conflict—or main problem—that the characters must solve. Write the conflict on the sticky note.

"The Princess and the Pea" by Hans Christian Andersen

There was once a Prince who wished to marry a Princess; but it would have to be a real Princess. The Prince traveled all over the world in hopes of finding such a lady; but there was always something wrong. Princesses he found in plenty; but he was never quite sure that they were real Princesses. It seemed to him that something was not quite right about each lady. At last he returned to his palace quite upset, because he wished so much to have a real Princess for his wife.

The conflict is that the Prince wants to marry a real Princess, but he can't seem to find one.

One evening a fearful storm arose. It thundered and lightninged, and the rain poured down from the sky in buckets. All at once there was a violent knocking at the door, and the old King, the Prince's father, went out himself to open it.

It was a Princess who was standing outside the door. But because of the rain and the wind, she was in a sad condition. The water trickled down from her hair, and her clothes were wet and ruined. But she said she was a real Princess.

"Ah! We shall soon see about that!" thought the old Queen-mother. Without saying a word, she went quietly into a bedroom, took all the bed-clothes off the bed, and put three little peas at the bottom of the bed. She then laid twenty mattresses one upon another over the three peas, and put twenty feather beds over the mattresses.

"The Princess and the Pea," by Hans Christian Andersen, continued

Upon this bed the Princess was to pass the night.

The next morning she was asked how she had slept. "Oh, very badly indeed!" she replied. "I have scarcely closed my eyes the whole night through. I do not know what was in my bed, but I had something hard under me, and am all over black and blue. It has hurt me so much!"

Now it was plain that the lady must be a real Princess, since she had been able to feel the three little peas through the twenty mattresses and twenty feather beds. None but a real Princess could have had such a delicate sense of feeling.

So the Prince took her for his wife, now that he knew she was a real Princess. And the three peas were placed in a museum, where they can still be seen, provided they are not lost.

Step 2: Note beginning, middle, and end.

Next, figure out the most important events in the plot.

Directions: Use a Story Organizer to record your thoughts.

Story Organizer

Beginning	Middle	End
A Prince travels the world looking for a real Princess to marry, but he has no luck. He returns home unhappy.	One night, during a terrible storm, a girl shows up at the palace. She says that she is a real Princess. The Queen-mother puts 3 peas under 20 mattresses and has the girl sleep on top as a test.	The next morning, the girl complains that the bed was lumpy—meaning she felt the peas. The Queen and Prince now believe that she is a real Princess. The Prince marries her.

Step 3: Keep track of the parts of a plot.

In most plots, events build to a climax. Then the problem is solved.
The plot can be diagrammed as a mountain.

Directions: Complete this Plot Diagram for "The Princess and
the Pea."

Plot Diagram

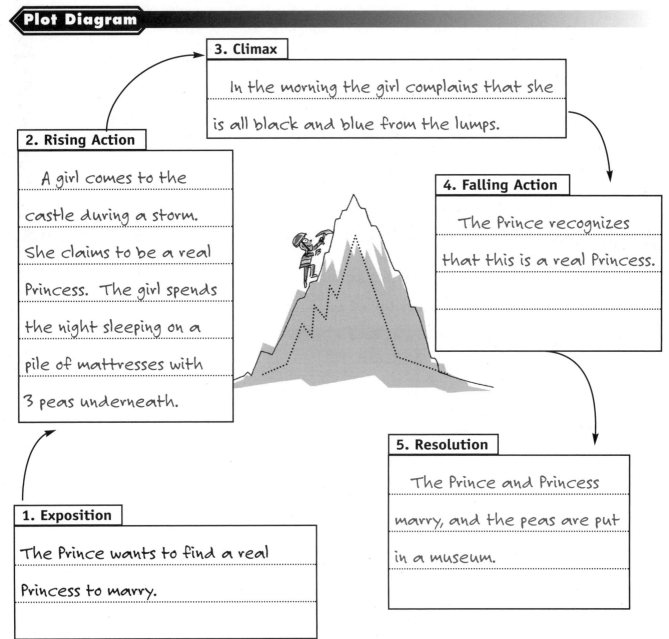

3. Climax

In the morning the girl complains that she
is all black and blue from the lumps.

2. Rising Action

A girl comes to the
castle during a storm.
She claims to be a real
Princess. The girl spends
the night sleeping on a
pile of mattresses with
3 peas underneath.

4. Falling Action

The Prince recognizes
that this is a real Princess.

1. Exposition

The Prince wants to find a real
Princess to marry.

5. Resolution

The Prince and Princess
marry, and the peas are put
in a museum.

Focus on **Theme**

A theme is the author's message about life. As a reader, you must make inferences about the author's theme. This three-step plan can help.

Step 1: Find the "big ideas."

Sometimes the title or first and last paragraphs of a work will give you clues about the "big ideas "or topics in the story.

Directions: Read the first and last paragraphs from this well-known book. Then write what you think the big, general ideas might be.

from the beginning of *Charlotte's Web* by E. B. White

"Where's Papa going with that ax?" said Fern to her mother as they were setting the table for breakfast.

"Out to the hoghouse," replied Mrs. Arable. "Some pigs were born last night."

"I don't see why he needs an ax," continued Fern, who was only eight.

"Well," said her mother, "one of the pigs is a runt. It's very small and weak, and it will never amount to anything. So your father has decided to do away with it."

"Do *away* with it?" shrieked Fern. "You mean *kill* it? Just because it's smaller than the others?"

Mrs. Arable put a pitcher of cream on the table. "Don't yell, Fern!" she said. "Your father is right. The pig would probably die anyway."

from the end of *Charlotte's Web* by E. B. White

Wilbur never forgot Charlotte. Although he loved her children and grandchildren dearly, none of the new spiders ever quite took her place in his heart. She was in a class by herself. It is not often that someone comes along who is a true friend and a good writer. Charlotte was both.

Big ideas: *death, being a "runt," friendship*

Fiction

Step 2: Look at what characters say or do.

Once you know what "big ideas" the work is about, look for what the characters say or do that relates to those ideas.

Directions: Read these quotes from *Charlotte's Web*. What do they say about friendship? Write your ideas in the right-hand column.

◄ **Double-entry Journal**

Quotes	My Thoughts
Wilbur didn't want food, he wanted love. He wanted a friend—someone who would play with him.	Friendship is just as important as food. A friend will love you and play with you.
"You're terrific as far as *I'm* concerned," replied Charlotte, sweetly, "and that's what counts. You're my best friend, and *I* think you're sensational."	Friends appreciate each other.
"Why did you do all this for me?" he asked. "I don't deserve it. I've never done anything for you." "You have been my friend," replied Charlotte. "That in itself is a tremendous thing."	It's a tremendous thing to be a friend. Friends help each other.

Step 3: Decide what the theme is.

A theme is what the author wants to tell you about life. It is what the author is saying *about* a big idea.

Directions: Use your ideas from Steps 1 and 2 to complete this diagram.

Theme Diagram

Step 1: What is the topic or big idea of the work?

friendship

Step 2. What do the characters say or do that relates to the topic?

| Wilbur wants a friend. | Charlotte thinks Wilbur is terrific. | Charlotte says that being a friend is a tremendous thing. |

Step 3: What does this tell you that is important to learn about life?

Friendship is one of the most important things in the world.

Fiction

Focus on Authors

Sometimes you'll want to become an "expert" on a particular author. This means that you will want to compare the author's books.

Step 1: Read.

Read two or more works by one author. Then choose an element to compare, such as characters, plot, setting, or theme. Here you'll compare characters.

Directions: Read these excerpts from two novels by Louis Sachar. Complete the sticky notes.

from *There's a Boy in the Girls' Bathroom* by Louis Sachar

Bradley Chalkers sat at his desk in the back of the room—last seat, last row. No one sat at the desk next to him or at the one in front of him. He was an island.

If he could have, he would have sat in the closet. Then he could shut the door so he wouldn't have to listen to Mrs. Ebbel. He didn't think she'd mind. She'd probably like it better that way too. So would the rest of the class. All in all, he thought everyone would be much happier if he sat in the closet, but unfortunately, his desk didn't fit.

> What I know about
>
> Bradley Chalkers:
>
> He wants to be left alone.
>
> He doesn't feel very good
>
> about himself. He thinks
>
> no one likes him.

from *Sideways Stories from Wayside School* by Louis Sachar

Jason had a small face and a big mouth. He had the second biggest mouth in Mrs. Jewls's class. And there were an awful lot of big mouths in that class.

"Mrs. Jewls," Jason called out without raising his hand. "Joy is chewing gum in class!"

Joy had the biggest mouth in Mrs. Jewls's class. And it was filled with gum. There was hardly even room for her tongue.

from *Sideways Stories from Wayside School* by Louis Sachar, continued

"Joy, I'm ashamed of you," said Mrs. Jewls. "I'm afraid I'll have to put your name up on the board."

"That's okay, Mrs. Jewls," Jason called. "I'll do it." Jason hopped out of his seat and wrote Joy's name on the blackboard under the word DISCIPLINE.

While he was up, Joy took the glob of gum out of her mouth and placed it on Jason's chair.

What I know about Joy:

She has a big mouth.

She breaks rules.

What I know about Jason:

He has a big mouth. He is a tattletale. He might be a teacher's pet.

Step 2: Draw conclusions about Sachar's characters.

Next, draw conclusions about the characters in the two novels.

Directions: Write notes about the three characters.

Inference Chart

Character	What I Know	What I Conclude
Bradley Chalkers	He wants to sit in the closet. He thinks no one likes him.	He doesn't feel good about himself. He wants to be left alone.
Jason	He has a big mouth. He is a tattletale.	He seems like he might be a goody-goody or a teacher's pet.
Joy	She was chewing gum in class. She put the gum on Jason's chair.	She gets even. She doesn't like tattletales.

Step 3: Compare and contrast characters.

After you read a few books by the same author, you will begin to notice the same type of characters popping up in the books. Comparing and contrasting characters from different books will help you begin to understand an author.

Directions: Complete this Venn Diagram to compare and contrast two characters from different Sachar novels.

Venn Diagram

Bradley

boy, wants to be alone, thinks no one likes him

Both

go to school, don't like school, don't fit in, have problems with other kids

Joy

girl, breaks rules, gets even

Step 4: Report.

What similarities do you see in Sachar's stories?

Directions: Write a journal entry about Bradley and Joy. Explain how the characters are similar.

Journal Entry

Bradley and Joy have a lot in common. They both go to school and have pretty strong opinions about it. They both seem to have problems with school or other kids. Bradley says no one likes him. Joy breaks class rules and gets tattled on. Both characters seem strong-willed. They know what they like and don't like.

Reading a Poem

A poem says a lot in just a few words. This is why you have to read every word very carefully. Your job when reading a poem is to "listen" to the music of the words and figure out what they mean. You can practice here.

Before Reading

Use the strategy of close reading to help you read a famous poem by William Wordsworth.

A Set a Purpose

Sometimes you read a poem for fun. Sometimes you read a poem for a class assignment. Either way, you need to figure out what the poem is saying. Make that your purpose for reading.

• **To set your purpose, ask a question about the meaning of the poem or the things that make it special.**

Directions: Write a purpose question for reading Wordsworth's "The Kitten at Play." Then tell how you feel about reading poetry. What's easy about it? What's difficult?

Purpose question: What is "The Kitten at Play" about?

This is what's easy about reading poetry: Sample response: If the poem has rhyme, it's easier to read. Plus, the words need to be simple enough to understand without a dictionary.

This is what's hard: Sometimes I have a hard time figuring out what the poet is trying to say.

Poetry

B Preview

It's important that you preview a poem before reading it. Look at the title and the poet's name. Check for rhyme and repeated words. Then read the first and last lines carefully.

Directions: Preview the poem on the next page. Make notes on this chart.

Preview Notes

The title of the poem is: *"The Kitten at Play"*

The poet's name is: *William Wordsworth*

This is what I noticed about the shape of the poem: *The lines are short. It's divided into four parts, or stanzas. It's not a very long poem.*

This is what came to mind when I read the first line: *It made me wonder how a kitten could be on a wall.*

This is what I noticed when I read the last line: *The kitten's name must be Tabby.*

I saw these rhyming words: *wall/fall; three/tree; air/fair; and so on*

I saw these repeated words: *"See the kitten"*

From my preview, I learned that this poem is about *watching a kitten play.*

"The Kitten at Play" by William Wordsworth

See the kitten on the wall,
Sporting with the leaves that fall,
Withered leaves, one, two, and three
Falling from the elder tree,
Through the calm and frosty air
Of this morning bright and fair.

Stop and Record

Who and what does this poem describe? Make some notes on the second Reading a Poem Chart (page 131).

See the kitten, how she starts,
Crouches, stretches, paws, and darts
With a tiger-leap half way
Now she meets her coming prey.
Lets it go as fast and then
Has it in her power again.

Stop and Record

What is the kitten doing? Make some notes on the second Reading a Poem Chart (page 131).

Now she works with three and four,
Like an Indian conjurer;
Quick as he in feats of art,
Gracefully she plays her part;
Yet were gazing thousands there,
What would little Tabby care?

Stop and Record

What do you know about the kitten? Make some notes on the second Reading a Poem Chart (page 131).

Poetry

C Plan

The strategy of close reading can help you understand the meaning of the poem. Careful reading of poetry usually means reading a poem at least three times.

> • **When you do a close reading of a poem, you think about every word and phrase.**

During Reading

D Read with a Purpose

On your first reading, read for fun. On your second reading, think about the meaning of the poem. On your third reading, look for important elements such as rhyme and rhythm. Listen for the "sound" of the poem.

Third Reading

Question	My Answer
What rhyming words did you see?	wall/fall; three/tree; air/fair, and so on
What is the rhythm, or "beat," of this poem?	The poem sounds sort of bouncy. I feel like reading it really fast—almost as fast as a kitten moves.

Directions: Read Wordsworth's poem three times. Make notes on the charts that follow.

Reading a Poem Charts

First Reading

Question	My Answer
What did you like about the poem?	I like how friendly it seems. The poet makes it easy to picture this playful little kitten.
What did it remind you of?	The poem reminded me of my grandmother's cat. She runs around a lot, just like this kitten.
Was there anything you didn't understand?	I had a hard time understanding some of the words, like "conjurer."

Second Reading

Question	My Answer
Who and what does this poem describe?	A kitten is playing. It's a cold, sunny morning with leaves falling from the trees.
What is the kitten doing?	She's playing with fallen leaves, pouncing on them.
What do you know about the kitten?	She's playful, fast, energetic, and concentrating on her game.

Poetry

Using the Strategy

The best strategy to use with a poem is a close reading.

• Record your close reading ideas on a Two Per Line chart.

Directions: Read this stanza from the poem. Circle two important words in each line. Write your ideas about each line.

Two Per Line

Text	My Ideas
See the (kitten) how she (starts)	The kitten is about to do something—probably play.
(Crouches) stretches, (paws,) and darts	She's ready to attack something. Watch out!
With a (tiger-leap) half way	Comparing her to a tiger makes her sound ferocious. She jumps really high.
Now she (meets) her coming (prey.)	"Prey" is an enemy you want to kill. Her "prey" is the leaves. She wants to kill the leaves.
Lets it (go) as (fast) and then	A cat will catch a mouse, let it go, and then catch it again, for fun.
Has it in (her power) again.	"Power"—another scary word.

Understanding How Poems Are Organized

Poets make all kinds of choices. Here are two of the most important:

1. To write with or without rhyme

2. To write with shape and structure or without

Directions: Do a close reading of this stanza. Then answer the questions. Look back at the entire poem if you need to.

> **from "The Kitten at Play" by William Wordsworth**
>
> See the kitten, how she starts,
> Crouches, stretches, paws, and darts
> With a tiger-leap half way
> Now she meets her coming prey.
> Lets it go as fast and then
> Has it in her power again.

The rhyming words in this stanza are starts/darts, way/prey, then/again

The pattern is that line 1 of each stanza always rhymes with line   2 .

The poem has 4 stanzas.

The stanza above is number 2   in the poem.

E Connect

When you read a poem, tune into your feelings.

• **Think about how the poem connects with your own experiences.**

Poetry

Directions: Answer these questions about the poem.

Connecting to a Poem

> The kitten in Wordsworth's poem makes me feel happy. I love all kinds of baby animals. I could watch them play for hours.

> The kitten reminds me of my grandmother's cat because that cat never sits still either!

After Reading

Take a moment to collect your thoughts about "The Kitten at Play."

F Pause and Reflect

Reread the purpose question you wrote on page 127.

- **After you finish a poem, ask yourself, "How well did I meet my purpose?"**

Directions: Tell why you have or have not met your reading purpose.

I feel I have met my purpose. I understand this poem really well.

G Reread

If the meaning of the poem is still not clear to you, you'll need to do some rereading. Use the strategy of paraphrasing. It can help you see a poem more clearly.

- **A powerful rereading strategy to use with poetry is paraphrasing.**

Directions: Rewrite the lines below in your own words. Then write your thoughts about the lines. Look up any words you don't know in a dictionary. Note that a *conjurer* is a magician or a juggler.

Paraphrase Chart

Lines	My Paraphrase	My Thoughts
"Now she works with three and four, / Like an Indian conjurer;"	The kitten juggles 3 or 4 leaves like a magician or juggler.	This kitten is tossing leaves in the air; she is really talented.
"Quick as he in feats of art, / "Gracefully she plays her part."	She is just as fast as a juggler, but much happier.	It looks hard, but the kitten is having a wonderful time.
"Yet were gazing thousands there, / What would little Tabby care?"	Even if thousands of people were watching, the kitten wouldn't care.	The kitten is totally wrapped up in her own game.

H Remember

It's easy to remember a poem if it means something special to you.

• **Writing your own version of a poem can help you remember it.**

Directions: On the lines below, write a poem called "The Puppy at Play." Your poem can be as long or short as you like.

See the puppy chase the ball,

Running, jumping, and then a fall,

But up he jumps—one—two—and three—

Ball keeps rolling, rolling: Whee!

Down the long and bumpy drive,

Puppy can't let it pass by.

Focus on Language

In a poem, every word counts. When you read a poem, look closely at the poet's use of language. Note the special ways that words are used.

Step 1: Read and take notes.

Begin by reading the poem the whole way through without stopping. Then read it a second time. Pay attention to words that seem important or unusual.

Directions: The poem below was written in honor of the Statue of Liberty. As you read it, circle words or phrases that seem important. Underline words you don't know.

"The New Colossus" by Emma Lazarus

Not like the brazen giant of Greek fame,
With conquering limbs astride from land to land;
Here at our sea-washed, sunset gates shall stand
A mighty woman with a torch, whose flame
Is the imprisoned lightning, and her name
Mother of Exiles. From her beacon-hand
Glows world-wide welcome; her mild eyes command
The air-bridged harbor that twin cities frame.
"Keep ancient lands, your storied pomp!" cries she
With silent lips. "Give me your tired, your poor,
Your huddled masses yearning to be free,
The wretched refuse of your teeming shore.
Send these, the homeless, tempest-tost to me,
I lift my lamp beside the golden door!"

Step 2: Find key words.

As a second step, read the poem again. Focus on the key words. Be sure you understand their meanings.

Directions: Reread "The New Colossus." Write a short definition for each word or phrase below. If necessary, use a dictionary. The first one has been done for you.

Colossus: a giant statue of a god that stood at the harbor entrance of an ancient Greek city

torch: a light to be carried around

exiles: people forced to leave their homes and countries

beacon: a light used as a signal

huddled masses: large groups of people crowded together

wretched refuse: miserable waste or cast-off garbage

Step 3: Look for figurative language.

Most poems contain figurative language.

Directions: Review page 313 in your *Reader's Handbook*. Then find two examples of figurative language in "The New Colossus." Write them on the chart.

Metaphor	Personification
• the Statue of Liberty as a "mighty woman with a torch"	• the Colossus as a "brazen giant"
• the flame of the torch as "imprisoned lightning"	• the Statue of Liberty as a woman who speaks with silent lips and lifts her lamp

Poetry

Step 4: Understand the images.

Poets use images to appeal to your senses. Images can help you really "see" the things the poet describes.

Directions: Look at these images from the poem. Tell what you think each one means. Then tell what sense or senses they appeal to.

Image in the Poem	What I Think It Means	What Senses I Use (sight, sound, smell, touch, or taste)
"our sea-washed, sunset gates"	The gates to the U.S. are through the NY harbor, washed by the sea and sun.	sight, sound, touch
"From her beacon-hand / Glows world-wide welcome"	The light that the Statue of Liberty holds up welcomes people to the U.S.	sight
"The wretched refuse of your teeming shore."	The miserable outcasts of your crowded countries.	sight, smell, touch

Step 5: Note how it affects you.

Ask yourself how the language of the poem affected you.

Directions: Write a journal entry about the poem "The New Colossus." Tell what feelings you had when you read the poem. Which image stirred you the most?

Journal Entry

I felt proud to be an American as I read the poem. I could picture all those poor, tired people coming to this country for a better life. My great-grandparents were some of those people. I feel proud to live in a country that welcomes all people.

NAME

Focus on Meaning

To understand a poem's meaning, you need to look at each word and understand every line. Follow these steps to focus on a poem's meaning.

Step 1: Read for the subject.

As a first step, read the poem the whole way through without stopping. Try to get an idea of what it is about.

Directions: Read "The Sleepy Giant." Write ideas on the sticky note.

"The Sleepy Giant" by Charles E. Carryl

My age is three hundred and seventy-two,
    And I think, with the deepest regret,
How I used to pick up and voraciously chew
    The dear little boys whom I met.

I've eaten them raw, in their holiday suits;
    I've eaten them curried with rice;
I've eaten them baked, in their jackets and boots,
    And found them exceedingly nice.

But now that my jaws are too weak for such fare,
    I think it exceedingly rude
To do such a thing, when I'm quite well aware
    Little boys do not like to be chewed.

And so I contentedly live upon eels,
    And try to do nothing amiss,
And I pass all the time I can spare from my meals
    In innocent slumber—like this.

This poem is about: a giant who used to eat boys but has changed his ways. I noticed these repeated words: little boys, I, I've, eaten

Poetry

Step 2: Read each word and each line.

Next, look closely at the key words and phrases of a poem.

Directions: Circle two key words in each line of the poem printed below. Then tell what the words mean and how they make you feel.

◄ Two Per Line ►

Text	My Ideas
My (age) is (three hundred) and seventy-two,	The giant is old.
And I think, with the (deepest) (regret),	He is sorry for what he used to do.
How I used to (pick up) and voraciously (chew)	He loved to eat little boys.
The (dear) little (boys) whom I met.	It's funny to think of this giant feeling bad about how he used to eat little boys.
And so I (contentedly) live upon (eels,)	He eats eels—I guess eels are soft and easy to eat. (Yuck!)
And try to do (nothing) (amiss,)	These days he tries to be good.
And I (pass) all the (time) I can spare from my meals	He spends all his time eating and sleeping.
In (innocent) (slumber)—like this.	He calls himself "innocent."
	I guess he feels sorry for eating those boys, but mostly he just sounds too tired to try anymore.

Step 3: Connect.

Pay attention to how the words of a poem make you feel. This can help you find the poem's meaning.

Directions: Answer this question about "The Sleepy Giant."

How did you feel as you were reading the poem? I felt happy. I like the poem because it's funny and a little bit silly.

Step 4: State the poem's meaning.

The meaning of a poem is not always obvious. Ask yourself, "What is the poet trying to say?"

Directions: Write the subject of "The Sleepy Giant." Then tell what you think the poem means.

Subject of the poem: an old giant who has stopped eating little boys

The statement the poet is making: Some possibilities: Even a very old giant can change his ways. OR It's easy to give up a bad habit when you get old and tired.

Poetry

Focus on Sound and Shape

Studying the sound and shape of a poem can give you clues about its meaning. Follow these steps to examine the rhyme, rhythm, and organization of a poem.

Step 1: Listen for rhyme.

On your first reading, listen for words that rhyme.

Directions: Read "The Months." Write what you notice about the rhymes on the sticky notes.

"The Months" by Sara Coleridge

January brings the snow,
Makes our feet and fingers glow.

February brings the rain,
Thaws the frozen lake again.

March brings breezes loud and shrill,
Stirs the dancing daffodil.

April brings the primrose sweet,
Scatters daisies at their feet.

May brings flocks of pretty lambs,
Skipping by their fleecy dams.

June brings tulips, lilies, roses,
Fills the children's hands with posies.

These words rhyme in the first 6 stanzas: snow/glow; rain/again; shrill/daffodil; sweet/feet; lambs/dams; roses/posies

NAME _____

"The Months" by Sara Coleridge

Hot July brings cooling showers,
Apricots and gillyflowers.

August brings the sheaves of corn,
Then the harvest home is borne.

Warm September brings the fruit,
Sportsmen then begin to shoot.

Fresh October brings the pheasant,
Then to gather nuts is pleasant.

Dull November brings the blast,
Then the leaves are whirling fast.

Chill December brings the sleet,
Blazing fire and Christmas treat.

These words rhyme in the final 6 stanzas:

showers/gillyflowers;

corn/borne; fruit/shoot;

pheasant/pleasant;

blast/fast; sleet/treat

Step 2: Hear the rhythm.

After you've examined the rhyme, reread the poem. Listen for the rhythm or "beat."

Directions: Reread page 325 in the *Reader's Handbook*. Then mark the stressed and unstressed syllables in these four lines from "The Months." Tell what the poem sounds like to you.

Listening for Rhythm

/ ⌣ / ⌣ / ⌣ /
January brings the snow,

/ ⌣ / ⌣ / ⌣ /
Makes our feet and fingers glow.

/ ⌣ / ⌣ / ⌣ /
February brings the rain,

/ ⌣ / ⌣ / ⌣ /
Thaws the frozen lake again.

This poem sounds like a nursery rhyme for children or a chant a teacher or parent might use to teach the names of the months.

Poetry

Step 3: Consider the shape and organization.

To understand a poem's shape and organization, try using a graphic organizer.

Directions: Make notes about Coleridge's poem on the calendar page below.

Calendar Organizer

Year-at-a-Glance

Write the name of the month at the top.

Write notes from Coleridge's poem underneath.

January	February	March	April
snow, glowing feet and fingers	rain, thaws frozen lake	breezes, daffodils	primroses and daisies
May	June	July	August
lambs	tulips, lilacs, roses, posies	showers, apricots, gillyflowers	corn, harvest
September	October	November	December
fruit, sportsmen shooting	pheasant, nuts	blast, leaves	sleet, fires, Christmas

Reading a  Play

*When you read a play, "listen" to the characters' voices.
Try to picture what's happening on stage. You can
practice here.*

Before Reading

Use the reading process and the strategy of summarizing to help you
read the play *Pinocchio*.

A Set a Purpose

Your purpose for reading a play is to find out about the characters,
setting, plot, and theme.

• **To set your purpose, ask three questions about the play.**

Directions: Write three purpose questions for reading *Pinocchio* here.
Then tell what you already know about this story.

Purpose question #1 Who are the characters in the play, and what are they like?

Purpose question #2 What is the story all about? OR What happens?

Purpose question #3 What is the theme of Pinocchio?

What I know about the story: It's about a puppet whose nose grows longer when he
lies.

Drama

B Preview

When you preview a play, look at the title, cast of characters, and setting.

- **Previewing a play helps you know what to expect when it comes time to read.**

Directions: Preview this title page for *Pinocchio*. Complete the sticky notes.

Pinocchio

A Play Based on *The Adventures of Pinocchio*

by Carlo Collodi

Cast of Characters

Major
- Pinocchio, a wooden boy
- Geppetto, his adoptive father

Minor
- a boy
- musicians with horns and drums

Setting

Time: long ago

Place: a small village in Italy. Action takes place inside Geppetto's cottage and on the street in front.

The title of the play is Pinocchio.

These are the main characters:

Pinocchio and

Geppetto

This is how I picture the setting: It's a cute little village with cobblestone streets and cottages with straw roofs.

NAME ....

FOR USE WITH PAGES 348–366

from *Pinocchio*

PINOCCHIO is a puppet who was carved out of wood by a lonely old man named GEPPETTO. GEPPETTO loves the puppet so much that he begins to wish PINOCCHIO would come to life. One morning, GEPPETTO awakens to find that PINOCCHIO has come to life, although he is not exactly the "real boy" that GEPPETTO had hoped for. Still, GEPPETTO loves him and decides to teach him how to be good.

Act II, Scene 1

(PINOCCHIO *and his father, GEPPETTO, stand in the main room of their little cottage, which also serves as GEPPETTO's workroom. There are wood blocks and shavings all around, in addition to little jars of paint and assorted brushes. PINOCCHIO's feet are gone because he has been naughty.)*

PINOCCHIO *(Begging):* Dear father, if you make me some new feet, I promise to go to school, and study, and do my best as a good boy should. . . .

GEPPETTO *(Gently):* Boys always sing that song when they want their own will.

PINOCCHIO: But I am not like other boys! I am better than all of them, and I always tell the truth. I promise you, Father, that I'll learn a trade, and I'll be a comfort to you in your old age.

GEPPETTO *(Sadly):* Pinocchio, my son. I cannot stand to see you in this state. I will make you two new feet, if you promise to be good this time. . . .

(GEPPETTO *takes up his tools and two pieces of wood and sets to work. In less than an hour, the feet are finished—two slender, nimble little feet, strong and quick, modeled as if by an artist's hands.)*

GEPPETTO *(With love):* Close your eyes and sleep, now, my boy.

(PINOCCHIO *closes his eyes and pretends to be asleep. GEPPETTO sticks on his two new feet with a bit of glue melted in an eggshell. He works slowly and carefully so that the new feet look perfect.)*

GEPPETTO: There now, Pinocchio. Good as new.

PINOCCHIO *(Jumping from the table in great joy):* To show you how grateful I am to you, Father, I'll go to school now. But to go to school, I need a suit of clothes.

Drama

from *Pinocchio,* continued

Stop and Record

Fill in the "Beginning" section of your Story Organizer (page 151).

GEPPETTO *(Sadly):* Pinocchio, I don't have a penny in my pocket to buy a suit. But I knew this day was coming, so here is a suit for you that I've made myself, and shoes as well. *(Holds up a little suit made of flowered paper and a pair of shoes made from the bark of the tree.)* Will this do for you, my son?

PINOCCHIO: Yes Father! Now I will look like a gentleman.

GEPPETTO *(Quickly):* I'm sure you will. But remember, Pinocchio, that fine clothes do not make the man unless they be neat and clean.

PINOCCHIO: Very true. But, in order to go to school, I still need one more thing.

GEPPETTO *(Worriedly):* What is it, my son?

PINOCCHIO: An A-B-C book.

GEPPETTO: To be sure! You do indeed! But how shall we get a book like this?

PINOCCHIO: That's easy. We'll go to a bookstore and buy it.

GEPPETTO: And the money?

PINOCCHIO *(Ashamed):* I have none.

GEPPETTO *(Sadly):* Neither have I.

(PINOCCHIO, although usually a happy boy, becomes very sad at these words, and looks as if he might cry.)

GEPPETTO *(Upon seeing his son's face):* But wait! I have an idea! Just give me an hour, my son!

(GEPPETTO jumps from his chair, throws on his shabby, old jacket, and runs out of the house without another word. PINOCCHIO walks around the little cottage on his new feet, kicking the shabby furniture in great sadness.)

PINOCCHIO *(Strongly):* I won't go to school without an A-B-C book. I don't care what I promised Father. I won't!

(Suddenly, the door is flung open. GEPPETTO runs back in, a book in his hand. He is wearing only his shirt now, and his shoulders and hair are covered with snow.)

⬡ **from Pinocchio, continued**

GEPPETTO *(Shivering):* Pinocchio, I have returned. And look what I have brought for you!

(GEPPETTO holds out an A-B-C book to PINOCCHIO.)

PINOCCHIO *(Looking at the book, and then his father):* But where's your coat, Father?

GEPPETTO *(Gladly):* I have sold it.

PINOCCHIO: Why did you sell your coat?

GEPPETTO: It was too warm. I have no need for it. But look here, now you have a book for school!

(PINOCCHIO understands what his father has done, and jumps into the old man's arms. He kisses him over and over, so glad and grateful he is to have a new A-B-C book.)

Act II, Scene 2

(It is early the next day. PINOCCHIO is outside on the street in front of GEPPETTO's house. He begins walking toward school, whispering to himself all the while.)

PINOCCHIO *(Softly):* In school today, I'll learn to read, tomorrow to write, and the day after tomorrow I'll do arithmetic. Then, clever as I am, I can earn a lot of money. With the very first pennies I make, I'll buy Father a new cloth coat. Cloth, did I say? No, it shall be of gold and silver with diamond buttons. That poor man certainly deserves it. After all, isn't he in his shirt sleeves because he was good enough to buy a book for me? On this cold day, too! Fathers are indeed good to their children!

(From the distance, there is the sound of horns and drums: pi-pi-pi, pi-pi-pi . . . zum, zum, zum, zum.)

Stop and Record
Fill in the "Middle" section of your Story Organizer (page 151).

Drama

from *Pinocchio*, continued

PINOCCHIO *(Stopping to listen):* What can that noise be? What a nuisance that I have to go to school! Otherwise. . . . *(He stops again, worried and puzzled.)* Well, should I go to school or should I follow that music? *(He pauses for another moment, and then his face lights up with a big smile.)* Well! Today I'll follow the music, and tomorrow I'll go to school. There's always plenty of time for me to go to school!

(With that, PINOCCHIO runs towards the sound of the horns and drums. He stops in front of the musicians and sees a boy who is standing and staring at a big sign.)

PINOCCHIO *(To the boy):* What is this place?

BOY *(In a hushed voice):* It's the GREAT MARIONETTE THEATER.

PINOCCHIO: What time does the show start?

BOY: It is starting now.

PINOCCHIO: And how much does one pay to get in?

BOY *(Who is growing tired of Pinocchio's questions):* Four pennies.

PINOCCHIO *(Earnestly):* Will you give me four pennies until tomorrow?

BOY *(Mockingly):* I'd give them to you gladly, but just now I can't give them to you.

PINOCCHIO *(Pleading):* For the price of four pennies, I'll sell you my coat.

BOY *(Laughing):* If it rains, what shall I do with a coat of flowered paper? I could not take it off again.

PINOCCHIO: Do you want to buy my shoes?

BOY *(Looking down at the shoes made of bark):* They are only good enough to light a fire with.

PINOCCHIO: What about my hat?

BOY *(Irritated):* Fine bargain, indeed! A cap made of bread dough! The mice might come and eat it from my head!

PINOCCHIO *(Sadly):* Well, will you give me four pennies for this book?

(The BOY grabs the book from PINOCCHIO and looks carefully at its pages. After another moment, he hands four pennies to PINOCCHIO and turns to leave. PINOCCHIO stands in front of the theater, the four pennies in his hand. For a moment, he hesitates, remembering that GEPPETTO sold his coat to buy the A-B-C book. Then, with a happy little shrug, PINOCCHIO opens the theater door.)

Stop and Record

Fill in the "End" section of your Story Organizer (page 151).

NAME

Plan

Now make a plan. Choose a strategy that can help you understand
this play.

• **Use the strategy of summarizing to help you meet your
purpose for reading the play.**

During Reading

Do a careful reading of *Pinocchio*. Make notes as you go.

D Read with a Purpose

Use a Story Organizer to summarize the main events of the play.

Directions: Make notes on this Story Organizer as you read.

Story Organizer

Beginning	Middle	End
Pinocchio begs his father for a new set of feet. Geppetto agrees but asks Pinocchio to be good. When Pinocchio gets his new feet, he says that he will go to school now.	Pinocchio says that he needs clothes and an ABC book for school. Geppetto gives Pinocchio a suit made of paper and shoes made of bark, and he sells his own coat so that he can buy a book for his son. The next day, Pinocchio sets out for school.	On the way to school, Pinocchio hears horns and drums. He goes to listen and learns that a show is about to begin. Pinocchio ends up selling his ABC book for the money to get into the puppet theater.

Summarize the events here,   **here,**   **and here.**

Drama

Using the Strategy

To summarize a play, use your own words to tell the main events.

• **Summarizing can help you understand what you've read.**

Directions: Complete this Web. Think of details that are connected to the magnet word "Pinocchio." Then use the details to write a summary of what you've read.

Web

promises to
go to school

a wooden puppet
who has come to life

wants a suit
of clothes and a book

sells his new
book to see a show

Pinocchio

has great plans
for his life

skips school

runs off to hear
the music

Summary

Pinocchio is a puppet who has come to life. He promises his father he will go to school if his father makes him new feet. Then he asks for a suit of clothes and a book. As he goes to school, Pinocchio hears music and runs off, skipping school. Then he sells his new book for 4 pennies to see a show.

Understanding How Plays Are Organized

Most plays have several main parts called **acts.** Each act may be divided into several **scenes.** When the place or time changes, a new scene begins.

The plot of every play has a central conflict. (This is true for novels and stories, too.) The central conflict is the main problem the characters must solve.

- **To understand a play, note the setting of each scene and think about the central conflict.**

Directions: Make notes about the organization of *Pinocchio*. Then decide what the central conflict is. (Hint: It has to do with how Pinocchio behaves.)

This excerpt from *Pinocchio* starts with Act II. What do you think happened in Act I?

Pinocchio became a real boy, and he must have been naughty. Somehow he lost

his feet.

What is the place and time of Act II, Scene 1?   The place is the main room of

Geppetto's cottage. The time is long ago.

What is the place and time of Act II, Scene 2?   The place is outside on the street in

front of Geppetto's house. The time is early the next day.

The central conflict in *Pinocchio* is: Pinocchio promises to be good, but he ends up

being bad.

Drama

E Connect

When you read a play, make connections to your own life. Do the characters remind you of anyone you know? How do you feel about the characters?

• **Making a connection to a play can help you understand it.**

Directions: Make a personal connection to Pinocchio.

Pinocchio reminds me of the boy next door

because he's always in trouble. He's a nice kid, but he makes bad decisions all

the time.

Here's how I feel about Pinocchio: I think he is ungrateful and naughty. He

doesn't think about what he's doing. I don't like him much.

After Reading

When you finish reading, take a moment to think about the play.

F Pause and Reflect

Think about the details of the play you just read. Do you understand the characters, setting, plot, and theme of the play?

• **Ask yourself, "Have I met my purpose for reading?"**

Directions: Answer these questions about *Pinocchio*.

Who are the main characters, and what are they like? Pinocchio and Geppetto are the

main characters. Pinocchio is a naughty boy made of wood. He makes promises he

doesn't keep and gets in trouble. Geppetto is his loving father. He does many

things for his son.

What are some of the big ideas? being good; love between a parent and a child;

telling the truth.

NAME

 G Reread

Sometimes the theme of a play isn't clear at first. You may need to reread, asking the questions you might ask the author.

> • **Questioning the author can help you find the theme.**

Directions: Read the play for clues about how the author would answer the questions below. Then complete the diagram.

 **Theme Diagram**

Step 1. What are the big ideas in this play?

(being good)   (honesty)

Note: Another theme is love of family.

Step 2. What do the plot and characters tell you about these big ideas?

| Pinocchio promises he will go to school. | Pinocchio says he always tells the truth. | Pinocchio breaks his promise when he skips school. | Pinocchio is bad when he sells his book. |

Step 3. What point is the author trying to make?

Sometimes it's hard to be good.

 H Remember

Good readers remember what they've read.

> • **To remember a play, write about a key line.**

Directions: Write a key line from *Pinocchio*. Tell why it's important.

Key line: Sample answer: "Dear father, if you make me some new feet, I promise to go to school, and study, and do my best as a good boy should."

Why I chose it: It tells about big themes in the play: making promises, telling the truth, and being a good boy.

Focus on Language

One type of language in a play is called stage directions. *A second type is the* dialogue, *or conversation between characters. Follow these steps to understand the language of a play.*

Step 1: Read the stage directions.

Stage directions help you "see" the scene and picture what is happening in a play.

Directions: Read these stage directions. Then sketch the scene.

from *Pinocchio*

(PINOCCHIO *and his father,* GEPPETTO, *stand in the main room of their little cottage, which also serves as* GEPPETTO'S *workroom. There are wood blocks and shavings all around, in addition to little jars of paint and assorted brushes.*)

Sketch

Step 2: Think about the dialogue.

Dialogue tells you a lot about the characters. If you "listen" to what the characters say, you can find clues to their personalities.

Directions: Do a close reading of these lines. Then tell what you can conclude about the two characters from the dialogue.

---

from *Pinocchio*

PINOCCHIO *(Pleading):* Dear father, if you make me some new feet, I promise to go to school, and study, and do my best as a good boy should. . . .

GEPPETTO *(Gently):* Boys always sing that song when they want their own will.

PINOCCHIO: But I am not like other boys! I am better than all of them, and I always tell the truth. I promise you, Father, that I'll learn a trade, and I'll be a comfort to you in your old age.

GEPPETTO *(Sadly):* Pinocchio, my son. I cannot stand to see you in this state. I will make you two new feet, if you promise to be good this time. . . .

My inferences about Pinocchio: He is loving to his father

and he makes big promises. He thinks he is better than other boys.

....

....

....

My inferences about Geppetto: He is loving toward Pinocchio

and a little blind to Pinocchio's faults.

....

....

....

Drama

Step 3: Study key lines and speeches.

Studying a play's key lines and speeches can help you understand the play's characters and theme.

Directions: Do a close reading of the text below. Write two key quotes in the Double-entry Journal. Then write what you think they mean.

---

from *Pinocchio*

PINOCCHIO *(Softly):* In school today, I'll learn to read, tomorrow to write, and the day after tomorrow I'll do arithmetic. Then, clever as I am, I can earn a lot of money. With the very first pennies I make, I'll buy Father a new cloth coat. Cloth, did I say? No, it shall be of gold and silver with diamond buttons. That poor man certainly deserves it. After all, isn't he in his shirt sleeves because he was good enough to buy a book for me? On this cold day, too! Fathers are indeed good to their children!

(From the distance, there is the sound of horns and drums: pi-pi-pi, pi-pi-pi . . . zum, zum, zum, zum.)

PINOCCHIO *(Stopping to listen):* What can that noise be? What a nuisance that I have to go to school! Otherwise. . . . *(He stops again, worried and puzzled.)* Well, should I go to school or should I follow that music? *(He pauses for another moment, and then his face lights up with a big smile.)* Well! Today I'll follow the music, and tomorrow I'll go to school. There's always plenty of time for me to go to school!

Double-entry Journal

Quotes	My Thoughts
"With the very first pennies I make, I'll buy Father a new cloth coat."	Pinocchio loves his father and knows that his father is good to him.
"Well, should I go to school or should I follow that music?"	Pinocchio has to make a choice between doing the right or wrong thing.

Focus on  Theme

Most plays have themes. A theme is a statement about life. Follow these steps to find a play's themes.

Step 1: Find the subject or big idea.

The subject is what the play is about. A play might be about love, friendship, family, greed, honesty, or courage. To find the subject, ask yourself, "What is this play mostly talking about?"

Directions: Write two big ideas in *Pinocchio*.

Big Ideas in *Pinocchio*

Big Idea #1	Big Idea #2
choosing right over wrong; being good; honesty	love and family

Step 2: Tell what the characters do or say that relates to the big ideas.

Next, figure out the relationship between the characters and the big ideas. Pay attention to what the characters say and do.

Directions: Choose one big idea from Step 1. Tell what the characters in *Pinocchio* do or say that relates to the big idea.

Inference Chart

Big Idea: Example: choosing right from wrong

What Pinocchio says or does:	What this tells me about the theme:
Pinocchio says he will be good and go to school. He says, "Dear father, if you make me some new feet, I promise to go to school, and study, and do my best as a good boy should." But then he is naughty again almost the minute he steps out of the house.	It's hard to be good, even when you want to be.
What Geppetto says or does:	**What this tells me about the theme:**
Geppetto begs Pinocchio to be good. He seems to know that it is hard to be good. He says, "Boys always sing that song when they want their own will."	It is easy to say you will be good, but it's harder to follow through.

NAME ....

Step 3: Figure out the playwright's message.

Don't confuse a play's subject with its theme. The **subject** is what the play is about. The **theme** is the playwright's *message* about the subject.

Example

subject	+ what the author says about it	= theme statement
a father's love	+ a father makes sacrifices for his child	= A father's love is so strong that he will make sacrifices for his child.

Directions: Use this formula to find another theme in *Pinocchio*. Then write how you feel about the theme. Does it seem like a true statement about life?

subject	+ what the author says about it	= theme statement
choosing right from wrong	+ It's hard for Pinocchio.	= Choosing right from wrong can be hard sometimes.

How I feel about it: I think this is true. Sometimes I have to really stop myself from doing something bad. But everybody makes mistakes at times.

....

....

....

Drama

Reading a (Website)

There's so much to see and read on the Internet! It's easy to get lost exploring each link. It can be hard to stay on track and find the information you need.

Before Reading

Use the reading process and the strategy of reading critically to help you navigate a kids' reference website.

A Set a Purpose

Every library has a reference section—the section with dictionaries, encyclopedias, and other reference books. A lot of the same information is available on the World Wide Web. Suppose you found a website called "Reference Desk for Kids." Start by asking yourself, "Why am I at this site? What do I want to find out?"

• **To set your purpose, write questions about the subject.**

Directions: Use this K-W-L Chart to record what you already know and what you want to find out about Internet reference sites.

K-W-L Chart

What I **K**now	What I **W**ant to Know	What I **L**earned
Reference sites give answers.	What information will I find here?	This is a good place to go for reference books and
They can help you with a book report.	Which is better: a website or the library?	homework help. There are also some cool links
You can get facts and explanations.	Can I trust what I read on the Internet?	to other sites on the Internet.
Use this section to tell what you know about Internet reference sites.	List your questions about reference sites here.	Save this section for later, after you've visited the site.

B Preview

As soon as you arrive at a new website, do a quick preview. See if the site has the information you need.

• **Previewing a website lets you see what the site has to offer.**

Directions: Preview the Reference Desk website. Pay attention to the items on this checklist. Make notes on what you find.

Preview Checklist

Preview Items	My Notes	
✔ the site name and introductory information	Reference Desk for Kids; a library of reference books, plus links to other sites and a Homework Help Desk.	
✔ the main menu choices	dictionaries, thesaurus, synonym and antonym guides, encyclopedias, Homework Help Desk	
✔ the site's graphics and overall "look"	It looks like it's for kids. It looks easy to read.	
✔ the source, or who created and pays for the site	The Department of Education, State University, in Morningstar, New York. Dr. LaDonna Desmond, Ph.D., of State University is the director of the site.	
✔ links to other sites	Arts	Projects
	Authors Galore	Science and Math
	Computers	Study Guides
	History	Test Tips
	Literature	

Internet

http://www.referencedesk.com/kids.html*

Reference Desk
for Kids

Welcome to the Internet's most important reference site!

Parents sign in here

Kids sign in here

Reference Desk for Kids can help you find the information you need. We offer links to many different kids' sites on the Internet, in addition to our own library of must-have reference books. You can also use the Homework Help Desk for answers to your homework questions and study tips.

Search Referencedesk.com

Enter a question or keyword:

[   ]   **Go**

KIDS WANT TO KNOW!

Here are just a few of the topics kids have been asking about lately . . .

Crocodiles

NASA

Fast Food

Judy Blume

CLICK HERE TO SEE MORE

*URL is not real

NAME

http://www.referencedesk.com/kids.html*

Great Internet Links for Kids!

<u>Arts</u>

<u>Authors Galore</u>

<u>Computers</u>

<u>History</u>

<u>Literature</u>

<u>Projects</u>

<u>Science & Math</u>

<u>Study Guides</u>

<u>Test Tips</u>

Visit our Reference Room

Dictionaries

Search for a word in ours, or link to hundreds on the web!

Thesaurus

Your one-stop shop for brand new words.

Synonym and Antonym Guides

Big homework helpers!

Encyclopedias

Browse or search features. Plenty of cool graphics!

Homework Help Desk
Powered by AskMe

Enter your homework question here:

<u>Search tips</u>   **Ask Me**

A project of the Department of Education, State University, in Morningstar, New York. Dr. LaDonna Desmond, Ph.D., of State University is director of this site. Direct your comments to Dr. Desmond at <u>www.ldesmond@stateu/ny.edu/</u>

<u>click here for MORE ON THIS SITE</u>
Last updated: October 2002

*URL is not real

Internet

C Plan

Good readers ask themselves two important questions when reading a website:

• Does the site have the information I need? (If not, find another.)

• Can I trust the information I find? (Some sites give opinions, not facts.)

> • **Use the strategy of reading critically to evaluate a website and decide whether it is reliable.**

During Reading

Keep your reading purpose questions in front of you as you read. Use a Website Profiler to keep track of what you learn.

D Read with a Purpose

A Website Profiler gives basic information about a website. It can help you understand and evaluate the most important elements of the website.

Directions: Carefully read the Reference Desk for Kids website on pages 164–165.
Record your notes on the Website Profiler that follows.

◄ **Website Profiler**

Name: Reference Desk for Kids

Address (URL): http://www.referencedesk.com/kids.html

Sponsor — *Write who created the site here.*	Date — *Site last updated*
Department of Education, State University, Morningstar, NY	Oct. 2002

Point of View	**Expertise** — *Write the names of important people who work on the site here.*
It gives reference information for kids. Use it to look up facts for school or fun.	Dr. LaDonna Desmond, Ph.D., of State University directs the site.

Reaction

It has dictionaries, thesaurus, encyclopedias, plus a Homework Help Desk.

It also gives links to other Internet reference sites.

Write what you want to remember about the site here.

Internet

Using the Strategy

Reading critically means reading for answers to your questions. It also means deciding if you can trust the answers you find.

- **When you read critically, you decide which links will help you meet your purpose.**

Directions: Suppose you are working on a class project about recycling. Below are some Study Cards with questions you need to answer. Make some notes about the Reference Desk for Kids website on these cards.

Study Cards

What is recycling? What kinds of materials can be recycled?

Links I should follow:

Encyclopedias, Science & Math

Why?

I should find general information and good graphics.

Why is recycling important?

What are some good ideas for recycling projects?

Links I should follow:

Science & Math, Projects

Why?

Recycling is a science topic, and there may be some good ideas

for projects if I follow the "Projects" link.

Understanding How Websites Are Organized

A website really does look like a web. The spokes that reach out from the center of the web are paths or links that you can follow to other places on the Internet.

Directions: Complete this Web. List important links on the Reference Desk for Kids website. Then predict what you think you'll find there.

◄ **Web**

What I might find: word

meanings, spellings, pronunciations

What I might find: information on how to

do well on tests

Link to Dictionaries

Link to Science & Math

Reference Desk for Kids Site

Link to Test Tips

Link to Authors Galore

What I might find: information on

science & math topics

What I might find: information

about my favorite authors

Internet

E Connect

When you "connect" to a website, you react to what you read. You ask, "How do I feel about the information? Can I use what I've learned?"

- **Be sure to think about whether the website was of use to you.**

Directions: Write your reactions to the Reference Desk for Kids website in a journal entry.

Journal Entry

I think this website is pretty good. I like all the reference books it offers. I would come here to look up information for a school report. I also think I'd like to try the Homework Help Desk to see how that works. That could come in handy if I can't figure out a school assignment.

After Reading

Take your time when doing research on the Internet. Gather your thoughts about one site before linking on to the next.

F Pause and Reflect

Think about your original reading purpose.

- **After you visit a website, ask yourself, "How well did I meet my purpose? What else do I need to find out?"**

Directions: Return to the K-W-L Chart on page 162. Make some notes in the L column. Then explain what else you'd like to learn.

I need to find out more about the Homework Help Desk. I wonder how it works. Are there real people waiting to answer the questions kids type in? Or do other kids answer my questions?

NAME

 G **Reread**

Occasionally you may need to return to a site to double-check a fact or detail. You may also need to check the site to see if it is reliable.

• **A powerful rereading strategy to use with websites is skimming.**

<u>Directions:</u> Skim the website on pages 164–165 to help you answer these questions.

What is the source of the site?	What credentials does the site offer?	What is the purpose of the site?
The Department of Education, State University, in Morningstar, New York	Dr. LaDonna Desmond, Ph.D., of State University is director of the site.	The purpose is to help kids find the information they need.

Is this site reliable? Explain your answer.
I think that the information on this site must be reliable because there is a university involved.

 H **Remember**

Good Internet researchers remember what they've seen and learned.

• **To remember what you've learned, email a friend.**

<u>Directions:</u> Write an email to a friend recommending the site. Tell what the site has to offer and how it was helpful to you.

‹Email›

Hi Tam,

I found this great website on the Internet. It has all kinds of reference books, the same as the ones in the library. You can use it to help you research the report that's due next week. There is also a Homework Help Desk. That will come in handy. Here is the link: http://www.referencedesk.com/kids.html.

See ya, K.

Internet

Reading Tables and Graphs

You'll find tables and graphs wherever you find facts. Your job as a reader is to understand the information presented in the table or graph.

Before Reading

Use the reading process and the strategy of paraphrasing to help you understand tables and graphs.

A Set a Purpose

Your purpose for reading a table or graph might be to answer these two general questions: "What is this about?" and "What conclusions can I draw from it?"

• **To set your purpose, ask questions about the table or graph.**

Directions: A table and a graph are described below. Write two purpose questions for each one.

1. A bar graph about heavily forested U.S. states

Purpose question #1 *Which states have the most forests?*

Purpose question #2 *How many forests do these states have?*

2. A table on what kids like to eat at fast-food restaurants

Purpose question #1 *What do kids most like to eat at fast-food restaurants?*

Purpose question #2 *What conclusions can I draw from this information?*

NAME ....

B Preview

When you preview a table or graph, look at the words and the "picture."

• **Previewing can give you a general sense of what the graphic is about.**

Directions: Preview the bar graph on this page and the table on the next. Complete the Preview Notes.

Most Heavily Forested States

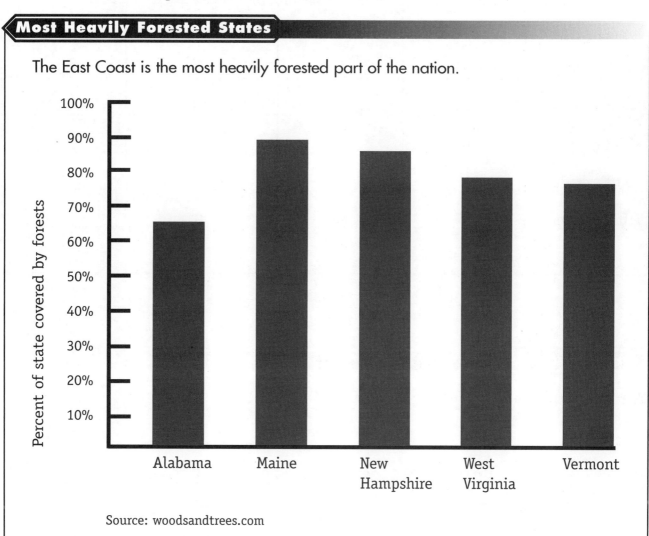

The East Coast is the most heavily forested part of the nation.

Percent of state covered by forests

Alabama Maine New Hampshire West Virginia Vermont

Source: woodsandtrees.com

Preview Notes

The title of the bar graph is: "Most Heavily Forested States."

The graph shows: which states have the most trees or forests.

The source for the graphic is: woodsandtrees.com

Graphics

173

Favorite Fast-Food Item

Forty children from each grade at Villa Rosa Elementary School were asked: "What is your favorite food item sold at a fast-food restaurant?" Here are the results.

Grade	Hamburger	Cheeseburger	Chicken Nuggets	Fries
Kindergartners	7	6	16	11
First graders	7	5	15	13
Second graders	10	7	11	12
Third graders	14	8	6	12
Fourth graders	20	12	1	7
Fifth graders	16	18	0	6

Source: *Fast Food News Magazine*

Preview Notes

The title of the table is: "Favorite Fast-Food Item."

The table shows: different kinds of food you eat at a fast-food restaurant and how many children in each grade prefer each one.

The source for the table is: Fast Food News Magazine.

C Plan

Your main job when reading a graphic is to pull together all of the data and then draw conclusions. The strategy of paraphrasing can help.

- **Paraphrasing can help you compare and contrast facts. It can also help you figure out what those facts mean.**

When you paraphrase, you use your own words to explain the most important details on the table or graph.

During Reading

Now do a careful reading of the bar graph and table.

D Read with a Purpose

Taking notes will help you absorb the most important details.

Directions: Write notes about the table and graph on these Paraphrase Charts.

Paraphrase Chart

Notes: "Most Heavily Forested States"	My Paraphrase
The subject is: which states have the most forests	The East Coast has the most forests. Ninety percent of Maine is covered in forests. The other states rank this way: New Hampshire, West Virginia, Vermont, and Alabama.
Key fact: Maine is the most heavily forested of any state in the country.	
Key fact: Eighty-six percent of New Hampshire is covered in forests.	
My thoughts: I'm surprised that 90% of Maine is covered in forests. That means there are very few towns and cities. I'm also surprised about the data for Alabama. I don't picture this as a big "tree state" at all.	

Graphics

Paraphrase Chart

Notes: "Favorite Fast-Food Item"	My Paraphrase
The subject is: foods that grade-school kids like the most at a fast-food restaurant.	This table shows that most kids in grades kindergarten through fifth grade like fries. Lots of young children also like chicken nuggets. Later, they switch to hamburgers and cheeseburgers.
Key fact: Really young children like fries and chicken nuggets the most.	
Key fact: The older children don't like chicken nuggets much.	

My thoughts: I kind of agree with what these kids said. I really liked nuggets and fries when I was little. But then I started choosing hamburgers over nuggets.

Using the Strategy

There are several different tools you can use to help you paraphrase. If a Paraphrase Chart doesn't work, try creating Summary Notes.

- Summary Notes can help you draw conclusions about information in a table or graph.

NAME

Directions: Write Summary Notes about the graph and table you just read.

Summary Notes

Title Most Heavily Forested States

Main Point The East Coast is the most heavily forested part of the nation.

Write what you think is the main point or idea here.

Detail 1	Detail 2	Detail 3
90% of Maine is covered in trees.	86% of New Hampshire is covered in trees.	79% of West Virginia is covered in trees.

List three smaller details that support the main idea here.

Title Favorite Fast-Food Item

Main Point As children get older, their fast-food choices change.

Write what you think is the main point or idea here.

Detail 1	Detail 2	Detail 3
Kindergartners prefer chicken nuggets to any other fast food.	By the third grade, more children prefer burgers over chicken nuggets.	Older children almost never call chicken nuggets their favorite anymore.

List three smaller details that support the main idea here.

Graphics

177

Understanding How Tables and Graphs Are Organized

Understanding the key parts of a table or graph is key to unlocking what it says.

Directions: Label the **title** and the **x-axis** and **y-axis** on the bar graph below. Then answer the question.

title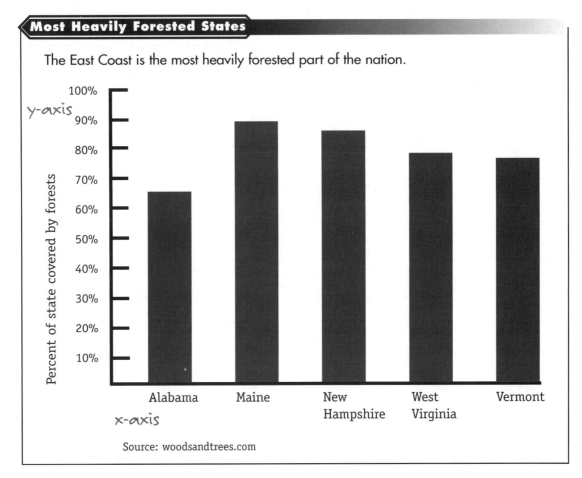

Most Heavily Forested States

The East Coast is the most heavily forested part of the nation.

y-axis

Percent of state covered by forests

Alabama   Maine   New Hampshire   West Virginia   Vermont

x-axis

Source: woodsandtrees.com

How would you find out how much of Vermont is covered by forests?

I would read across the bottom till I found "Vermont."

Then I would follow the bar up to the top. I would read across to the left to see

that 78% of Vermont is forested.

Connect

React to a table or graph after you finish reading it.

• **Use a Double-entry Journal to respond to the table.**

Directions: Fill in something you learned from the fast-food table on page 174. Then write your thoughts about what you learned.

Double-entry Journal

Information	My Thoughts and Feelings
Little kids like chicken nuggets and fries best, but older kids prefer burgers.	This is pretty much true for me, especially the part about the chicken nuggets. But I've loved fries from the very first time I tried them before kindergarten, and I still love them.

After Reading

After you finish paraphrasing and reacting to a table or graph, take a moment to look at it to make sure you haven't missed anything.

 Pause and Reflect

First, think back to your reading purpose.

• **Ask yourself, "How well did I meet my purpose?"**

Directions: Answer the questions below.

What is the bar graph on page 173 about? It shows which U.S. states are the most heavily forested and tells what percentage of each state is covered in woods.

What is the fast-food table on page 174 about? It shows which fast foods kids like most at different ages.

Can I draw conclusions from these graphics? I'm not sure.

Graphics

Reread

You may need to reread before you can draw conclusions from a table or graph.

> • **Use the rereading strategy of close reading to help you understand a table or graph.**

Directions: Do a close reading of the forest bar graph and the fast-food table on pages 173–174. Pay attention to every detail, and record your notes in the Summary Notes. Then answer the questions.

Summary Notes

Forest Bar Graph

The state with the most forests is Maine.

The state with the least forests is Alabama.

What percent of West Virginia is covered with forests? 79%

What percent of Maine is covered with forests? 90%

What is the main idea of this graph? The five most heavily forested states in the U.S. are Alabama, Maine, New Hampshire, West Virginia, and Vermont.

What can you conclude about Maine from this graph? Answers will vary. Examples: Maine must not have many cities or much industry. Maine must be a beautiful state. There must be a lot of good parks and camping in Maine.

What else would you like to know that the graph doesn't answer? Answers will vary. Example: I'd like to know what makes the East Coast a great part of the country for trees.

◀ **Summary Notes**

Fast-Food Table

How many kindergartners like chicken nuggets best? 16

How many first graders like chicken nuggets best? 15

How many fourth graders like chicken nuggets best? 1

How many kindergartners like fries best? 11

How many third graders like fries best? 12

How many fifth graders like fries best? 6

How many kindergartners like hamburgers best? 7

How many fourth graders like hamburgers best? 20

What fast food do fifth graders like best? cheeseburgers

Graphics

What is the main idea of this table? Young kids like chicken nuggets best, but by the time they're in 4th or 5th grade they prefer burgers.

What can you conclude about fries from this table?

Everyone seems to like fries, no matter what age they are.

What else would you like to know? Answers will vary. Example: What about kids who don't like any of the items listed? What do they like?

H Remember

It's easy to remember a graphic if you actually *do* something with the information.

• **To remember a graphic, graph it a different way.**

Directions: Use the numbers in the fast-food table to make a bar graph for the kindergartners. Draw the bar graph on this grid.

Bar Graph

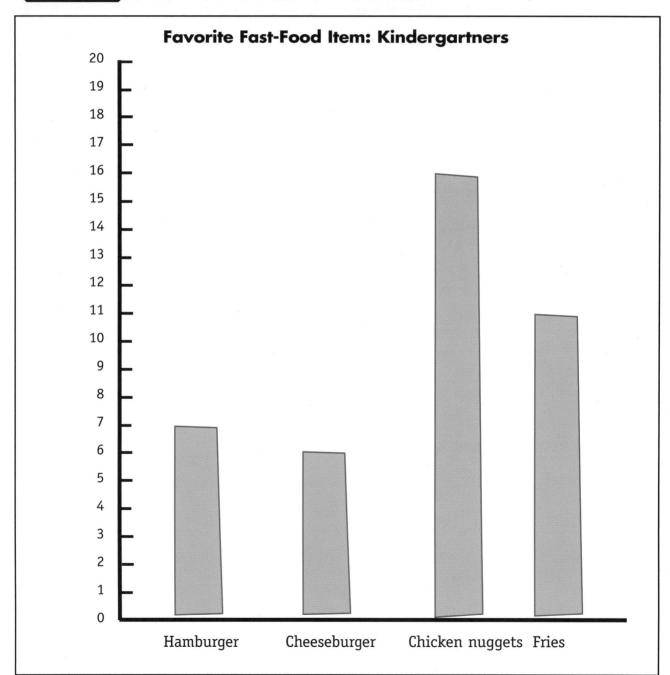

Favorite Fast-Food Item: Kindergartners

Reading a Test and Test Questions

The key to doing better on tests is to read carefully and use what you've learned. This plan can help.

Before Reading

Of course, your goal when taking a test is to get the answers right. Setting a purpose beforehand can help you meet this goal.

A Set a Purpose

Before starting a test, focus on your purpose.

- **Your purpose is to understand the test questions and find the information you need for the answers.**

Directions: For this sample test, you'll read an article about Colorado and then answer some test questions. Write your reading purpose here.

My purpose: Figure out what the test questions are about and then use the

article to help me answer them.

B Preview

As soon as you receive the test, begin previewing. This will help you know what to expect.

Directions: Look over the sample test that follows. Read the directions and take a quick look at the questions. Answer the questions on the Preview sticky notes.

Tests

Mid-Year Reading Test

Time: 60 Minutes

DIRECTIONS: Read the article "A History of Colorado" from *It Happened in America* by Lila Perl. Then answer each of the questions that follow.

A HISTORY OF COLORADO

Colorado is Spanish for "colored red." Spanish visitors of the 1500s gave this name to the Colorado River because it flows through gorges of reddish stone. Much of the state of Colorado lies in the Rocky Mountains, making it the nation's highest state on average. It has more than a thousand peaks that are over ten thousand feet high. And more than fifty of these soar to over fourteen thousand feet.

The spine of the Rockies, which zigzags through Colorado from north to south, forms part of the Continental Divide. West of the Divide, all waters flow toward the Pacific Ocean; east of the Divide, they drain toward the Atlantic.

Cliff-dwelling Indians lived in the Colorado region until the 1200s, when severe drought led to crop failures and drove them from their homes. In the 1600s and 1700s, both Spain and France laid claim to the area. Some of the present-day state of Colorado came to the United States through the Louisiana Purchase of 1803, and some was ceded after the Mexican War, in 1848. A gold strike in 1858 brought a rush of easterners, and the discovery of silver lodes in 1864 led to the nickname *The Silver State*.

Colorado is also nicknamed *The Centennial State* because it joined the Union in 1876, the year of the hundredth anniversary of the signing of the Declaration of Independence. . . . Although many early Colorado mining communities are now ghost towns, the state's mineral resources are still an important part of its economy.

Preview

How much time do you have to complete the test? 60 minutes

Preview

What is the reading passage about? It's an article about the history of Colorado.

Preview

What kinds of questions are there? There are 4 multiple-choice questions and 1 essay.

Mid-Year Reading Test, continued

Multiple-choice Questions

DIRECTIONS: Read each question and circle the letter of the correct answer. If you do not know an answer, make the best guess you can.

1. What kind of reading is "A History of Colorado"?
   A. fiction
   B. poetry
   C. nonfiction
   D. none of the above

   What does question #1 ask for? the kind of reading

2. Based on the reading, which of these statements is not true?
   A. The Rockies cover much of Colorado.
   B. Colorado has a long history of mining.
   C. Colorado is the highest state in the nation.
   D. Colorado was one of the first states to join the Union.

   What are the key words in #2? not true

3. What does the word *ceded* mean?
   A. handed over
   B. developed
   C. ruined
   D. divided

   Where is the word ceded in the article? in paragraph 3

4. What is the main idea of this article?
   A. *Colorado* is Spanish for "colored red."
   B. Colorado was once home to cliff-dwelling Indians.
   C. Colorado has a long and fascinating history.
   D. Colorado is known as the Centennial State.

   How I figured out the answer to #4: visualizing, thinking aloud, or summarizing

Essay Question

5. Imagine you are planning a trip to Colorado. What three places would you like to visit most? Support what you say with facts and details from the article.

   What is the topic of the essay? 3 places in Colorado I'd like to visit.

Tests

185

Plan

Now make a plan for taking the test.

Directions: Decide how much time you will need to complete each part of the test. Make notes on the chart.

Planning Chart

What to Do	Time I'll Spend
Read the selection.	10 minutes
Do multiple-choice questions.	20 minutes
Answer essay question.	20 minutes
Check answers.	10 minutes
Total time:	60 minutes

> Keep these time limits in mind as you take the test.

During Reading

After your preview, do a careful reading of the test passage and questions.

D Read with a Purpose

As you read, look for the most important ideas in each paragraph.

Directions: Read the article on Colorado. Underline one important sentence in each paragraph. Then highlight key words or phrases in the questions.

NAME

Using the Strategy

Your next step will be to choose a strategy that can help you answer the test questions.

• Use the strategy of skimming to find answers to test questions.

Skimming means glancing through a reading, searching for key words or phrases.

Directions: Read the four multiple-choice test questions on page 185. Write on the sticky notes by the questions. Then answer the questions. Skim the passage to help you find the answers.

Understanding How Tests Are Organized

Most tests are set up with the easy questions first. The most difficult questions usually come at the end. These questions may ask you to make connections between the beginning of a passage and the end.

Directions: Reread the essay question. Answer the question on the sticky note. Then explain what the question is asking for on the lines below.

The essay question is asking me to *choose three places in Colorado I'd like to visit*

and then use details from the passage to support what I say.

What facts from the passage will you need to write your essay? *facts on*

interesting places to visit in Colorado

E Connect

As often as possible, make personal connections to a test passage as you read.

• Use your thoughts and feelings to help you answer the essay question.

Tests

Directions: Complete the Main Idea Organizer below. First write the main idea by filling in the three blanks. Then write details that support the main idea. Remember that your details should come from the reading passage.

◀ **Main Idea Organizer**

Main Point On my trip to Colorado, I would like to visit		
• the Rocky Mountains		
• a gold or silver mine		
• a ghost town		
Detail 1	**Detail 2**	**Detail 3**
The Rocky Mountains cover much of the state and rise to very high peaks.	Minerals are an important resource in Colorado.	Colorado is filled with ghost towns. These towns were abandoned after the Gold Rush.

After Reading

After you complete a test, take a moment to gather your thoughts.

F Pause and Reflect

First, check that you've answered every question. Then ask yourself, "Have I answered each question to the best of my ability?"

- **After you finish a test, return to the questions that gave you the most difficulty and double-check your answers.**

This is the multiple-choice question that I found most difficult: the main idea question.

Here's why: I had to pull together all parts of the reading. This was pretty hard to do.

NAME

 G **Reread**

It's a good idea to return to the more difficult questions on the test.

• **A powerful rereading strategy to use is thinking aloud.**

Directions: Read this question. Then write a think-aloud that tells how you figured out the answer.

> **from Mid-Year Reading Test**
>
> 2. Based on the reading, which of these statements is not true?
>   A. The Rockies cover much of Colorado.
>   B. Colorado has a long history of mining.
>   C. Colorado is the highest state in the nation.
>   D. Colorado was one of the first states to join the Union.

Think Aloud

I skimmed the article to see if each statement was true. The article said that much of the state lies in the Rocky Mountains, so A is true. It said that gold mining started in 1858, so B is true. It says that Colorado is the nation's highest state, so C is true. It says that Colorado joined the Union 100 years after the signing of the Declaration of Independence, so it wasn't one of the first states to join the Union. So I know that D is the answer.

 H **Remember**

Take a look at your test after it's graded. Figure out what you did wrong so you can avoid making the same mistakes on future tests.

• **Remember the test questions that gave you trouble.**

Directions: Write what *you* can do to improve your test-taking ability.

I can improve my test-taking ability by 1. studying beforehand.

2. reading the test passage and questions slowly and carefully.

3. using the strategy of skimming.

Tests

Focus on Writing for Tests

Have you ever felt scared when you first spotted an essay question on a test? If so, you're not alone. But writing an essay for a test doesn't have to be hard. What you need is a plan.

Step 1: Read the directions.

Your first step will be to read the directions carefully—two times or more. Take note of key words and phrases.

Directions: Read these directions twice. Highlight key words. Then answer the questions.

> ### Sample Essay Question
>
> **DIRECTIONS:** Write a story about a fun family vacation. You may write about real events or a story that you make up. Write at least two paragraphs. Proofread your writing.

What type of writing will you do? a story

What is the topic of the writing? a fun family vacation

How long should it be? at least 2 paragraphs

Step 2: Plan your writing.

Start by choosing a fun family vacation you would like to write about. Then plan your story.

Directions: Make notes about your story on the organizer that follows.

Story Organizer

Topic Sample: A fun family vacation to Roaring Rapids Amusement Park		
Beginning	**Middle**	**End**
Last summer, my mom had no vacation plans. So I suggested Roaring Rapids Amusement Park.	Finally, my mom agreed to go. Our first day there, the park was empty! We went on every roller coaster. My mom got sick.	On the second day, we had to move more slowly. I went on lots of rides while my mom watched. It was the best vacation ever!

Step 3: Write your answer.

Your next step is to write your answer. Keep your organizer in front of you as you write.

Directions: Write the first paragraph of your family vacation story here.

On the first day of summer vacation, my Mom said, "We have no vacation plans for this summer." I told her that we had to take a vacation somewhere because everybody does. She said that if I chose a spot, planned the trip, and saved up my money for little expenses, then we could take a vacation. I could hardly wait to begin. I knew the best vacation spot in the world: Roaring Rapids Amusement Park, right in our own backyard!

Step 4: Check your writing.

As a final step, proofread your writing. Correct any spelling mistakes and problems with punctuation and capitalization that you see.

Directions: Proofread the paragraph you just wrote. Make corrections neatly.

Tests

Focus on Math Tests

Did you know that good readers often do well on math tests? Good reading skills will help you focus on the questions and figure out how to solve them.

Step 1: Read the directions and questions.

Your first step is to read the directions and questions. Underline key words and make notes if you can.

Directions: Read the sample math test question below. Highlight the key words in the directions and problem.

> **Sample Test Question**
>
> **DIRECTIONS:** Read and work each problem. Circle the letter of the correct answer.
>
> 1. A pet bird was taken away on a delivery truck by mistake. To get back home, it had to fly 950 kilometers. If the bird flew 15 kilometers a day for 60 days, how much farther would it still have to go?
>   A. 935 kilometers   C. 50 kilometers
>   B. 175 kilometers   D. 500 kilometers

Step 2: Decide how to solve the problem.

Use the strategy of thinking aloud to help you solve the problem.

Directions: Write a think-aloud that tells how you would solve the problem above.

> **Think Aloud**
>
> "How much farther" means how many more kilometers the bird has left to travel. To figure this out, I need to first figure out how much he has traveled thus far. Then I'll subtract that number from 950 kilometers, which is the total distance the bird needs to fly.

192

NAME

Step 3: Do the math.

Next, return to the problem and look at the choices. See if you can cross out one, two, or three answers that are clearly wrong. Then do the math.

Directions: Look at the question again. Cross out answers that are clearly wrong. Do an estimate. Then solve the problem.

Sample Test Question

1. A pet bird was taken away on a delivery truck by mistake. To get back home, it had to fly 950 kilometers. If the bird flew 15 kilometers a day for 60 days, how much farther would it still have to go?

~~A. 935 kilometers~~   C. 50 kilometers

B. 175 kilometers   ~~D. 500 kilometers~~

Think Aloud

To estimate, I'll change the 60 to a 6 because that number is easier to work with. 15 kilometers x 6 days = 90 kilometers, or 900 kilometers when I add back the zero. This is how much it's already traveled. I need to subtract that from 950. Now I'll do the math, but it looks like answer C is correct.

$60 \times 15 = 900$ $950 - 900 = 50$

Step 4: Check your answer.

Finish by checking your work. If you get stuck, try visualizing.

Directions: Make a sketch to show what the problem is asking for.

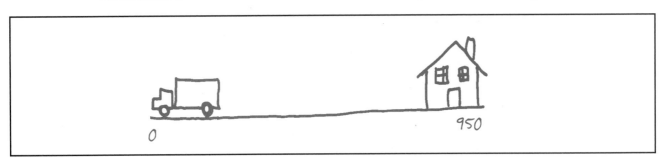

Tests

Focus on Science Tests

Reading skills will help you understand the questions and interpret the charts and tables on a science test.

Step 1: Read the question.

Take the time to read each question closely. Mark key words.

Directions: Read this sample question. Highlight the key words. Then complete the sticky note.

> **Sample Test Question**
>
> 1. What is the name of the molten rock that boils below the surface of a volcano?
>   A. vents   C. craters
>   B. lava   D. magma

For question #1, I need to figure out the name of the molten rock in a volcano.

Step 2: Find the answer.

Next, examine the choices and talk your way through the answer.

Directions: Read the answer choices for the question above. Then talk your way through to the answer. Make notes on the lines below.

> **Think Aloud**

I know that A and   C   are wrong because they are the names of parts of a volcano, not molten rock. I also think   B   is wrong because that's what flows down the front and sides of a volcano.

I'm going to say that the answer is D   .

194

Step 3: Draw conclusions from the graphics.

You might want to leave graphics questions for last, since these may take a little more time. When it's time to begin, study the graphic. See if you can figure out the big picture. Then read the questions. Go back to the chart or table and find the information you need.

Directions: Complete the sticky notes as you study this chart.

Sample Test Question

Tallest Mountains in North America

Peak	Location	Height in feet
McKinley	Alaska, USA	20,320
Logan	Yukon Territory, Canada	19,850
Citlaltepetl	Mexico	18,700
St. Elias	Alaska-Yukon	18,008
Popocatepetl	Mexico	17,887

2. Use the chart to decide which of these statements is not true.
   A. Logan is taller than St. Elias.
   B. The tallest mountain in the world is McKinley.
   C. St. Elias and McKinley share a home in Alaska.
   D. Popocatepetl is 17,887 feet tall.

The test question asks me to figure out which statement is not true.

The title of the chart is "Tallest Mountains in North America."

It shows the names of the five tallest mountains, their location, and their height in feet.

The answer is B because the chart shows only the tallest mountains in North America—not the whole world.

Tests

Focus on Social Studies Tests

Social studies tests focus on names and places, dates and events, and big ideas in history. On this type of test, you must read carefully and think critically. Follow these steps to improve your score.

Step 1: Read the questions.

Read each question carefully. Look for key words.

Directions: Read this sample test question. Highlight the key words.

> **Sample Test Question**
>
> 1. Which of these is an example of a natural resource?
>   A. plastics
>   B. people
>   C. cities
>   D. minerals

Step 2: Rule out answers that are obviously wrong.

If you don't know the right answer immediately, look for answers that you know are *wrong*. Cross them out and take a look at what you have left.

Directions: Return to the question above. Cross out the answers you know are wrong. Make notes here.

I know A and C   are wrong because natural resources are made by nature, and these two things are not.

NAME ....

Step 3: Talk your way through the answers.

Quietly think aloud the remaining answers to the question.

Directions: Complete this think-aloud.

Think Aloud

I think the answer might be D .... **because** minerals are something made by

nature that people can use, which is what a natural resource is.

Step 4: Draw conclusions from the graphics.

Read the title of a graphic first, to get an idea of the subject. Then read the questions. Find the information you need in the graph.

Directions: Read this pictograph and the questions on the next page. Complete the sticky notes. Then answer the questions.

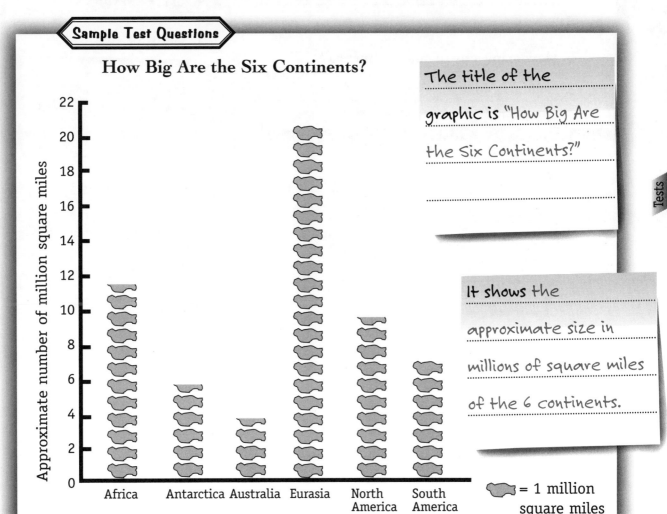

Sample Test Questions

How Big Are the Six Continents?

The title of the graphic is "How Big Are the Six Continents?"

It shows the approximate size in millions of square miles of the 6 continents.

= 1 million square miles

Tests

Sample Test Questions

DIRECTIONS: Use the pictograph to answer questions 2–5. Write your answers on the blanks.

2. Which continent is the largest in the world?

Eurasia

> To answer question 2, I need to find the continent with the most symbols and then read its name.

3. Which continent is the smallest?

Australia

> To answer question 3, I need to find the continent with the fewest symbols and read its name.

4. What does the map key show you?

each symbol stands for 1 million square miles

5. How many square miles is Eurasia?

21 million square miles

> To answer question 4, I need to find the map key in the bottom right-hand corner of the map.

> To answer question 5, I need to find the column for Eurasia and then trace my finger up the graph, counting the symbols.

Learning New Words

Words are something you can collect, like dolls or cars. You don't want just one or two—you want lots and lots of them. Collecting words helps build your vocabulary.

Step 1: Read.

As you read, collect new words.

Directions: Read this passage. Circle words that are unfamiliar to you.

from *Sojourner Truth: Ain't I a Woman?* by Patricia and Frederick McKissack

Colonel Hardenbergh noted the birth of another slave with the same indifference he might have shown a calf or a lamb. Whenever there was a slave birth, he went to see the mother and newborn in the quarters. "She has strong arms," he told the parents in Low Dutch. "She'll be a good worker."

Although Hardenbergh spoke English when conducting business, he still preferred speaking his ancestral Dutch at home. Besides, it was easier to control slaves who couldn't communicate with the majority of the people around them. So the first language the infant heard was Dutch, the language of her master.

Step 2: Record.

When you read a new word, write it down in your notebook. Remember to record where you first noticed the word.

Vocabulary

Directions: Write the words you circled on this notebook page.

Vocabulary Journal

Language Arts

from <u>Sojourner Truth</u>, p. 21

Unfamiliar Words	Definitions
indifference	disinterest; not caring
conducting	working at
preferred	chose as more desirable
ancestral	native; where you come from

Step 3: Define.

Use context clues or a dictionary to define every word on your list.

Directions: Get together with a partner. Working together, define the words on your list. Write the definitions on the chart above.

Step 4: Use new words.

The best way to remember a new word is to use it in conversation or in writing.

Directions: Working with your partner, write one sentence for each of the words you defined.

Practice Sentences

1. I saw indifference on the man's face, and I knew he didn't care.

2. Conducting personal business at work is a no-no.

3. She preferred her mother's cooking over her father's.

4. My abuela's ancestral home is Mexico.

NAME ....

FOR USE WITH PAGES 500-507

Building Vocabulary

What do you do when you come to an unfamiliar word?
You might guess and go. But if you really need to know
what the word means, try these strategies.

Step 1: Look at context clues.

You won't always have a dictionary at your side when you're reading.
So what's another way to find out the meaning of unfamiliar words?
Try using context clues.

Directions: Read the paragraph below. Use context clues to figure out
the meaning of the underlined words.

> ### from *Taking Sides* by Gary Soto
>
> He had moved from the Mission District of San Francisco, an <u>urban</u>
> barrio, to Sycamore, a pleasant suburban town with tree-lined streets. His
> mother had gotten tired of yanking open her <u>drapes</u> to see run-down Chevys
> and fender-buckled Ford Torinos bleeding black oil.

Underlined Words	My Definition	Context Clues
urban	city	The things the mother doesn't like all sound like things in a city. Also, they moved from the "urban barrio" to "a pleasant suburban town with tree-lined streets."
drapes	curtains	His mother is at the window yanking something open to see outside.

Vocabulary

Step 2: Use word parts.

If context clues don't work, try using word parts. Knowing roots, prefixes, and suffixes increases the number of words you understand.

Roots

Directions: Complete this Web with words that have the root *aud*.

auditorium

audience

aud = hear

audio

audible

Prefixes

Directions: Add a prefix from the box to each of the words on the list. Then tell what the word means.

| co- = together | tri- = three | mal- = bad |

Prefix + Word	New Word	Meaning of New Word
tri + cycle	tricycle	cycle with 3 wheels
mal + adjusted	maladjusted	not well adjusted
co + operate	cooperate	operate (work) together

Suffixes

Directions: Add suffixes to these words. Then use each word in a sentence.

| -ist = a person who | -less = without |

piano + -ist = pianist   Sentence: The pianist performed well.

thought + -less = thoughtless   Sentence: It was thoughtless of you to say you didn't

like her skirt.

Dictionary Dipping

Knowing the parts of a dictionary can help you find words quickly and efficiently.

Step 1: Read.

Use the guide words to help you find the word you're looking for. Once you've found the entry you need, read it carefully. Make notes to help you remember.

Directions: Read the definition for *entrap*. Then answer these questions about the entry.

> **Dictionary Entry**
>
> entertain • envelop
>
> **entrap** ĕn-trăp *verb.* **–trapped, -trapping** 1. To catch as if in a trap. 2. To lure into a dangerous situation. **Synonyms:** *catch, imprison*

How many definitions does *entrap* have? 2

What is the past tense form of the word? entrapped

What part of speech is *entrap?* verb

What are some synonyms for the word *entrap?* catch, imprison

Step 2: Remember.

The easiest way to remember a word is to use it over and over again.

Directions: Write a sentence using the word *entrap*.

Sentence: She was entrapped in her own lies.

Vocabulary

Understanding New Terms

You'll find many new words in your textbooks. These are known as "specialized terms." Each subject you learn about has its own specialized terms.

Step 1: Record.

Record each new word that you find. You can use a Concept Map to keep track of terms and their definitions.

Directions: Review the specialized terms in the "States and Boundaries" history article (pages 25–27). Write three of the terms on this Concept Map.

Concept Map

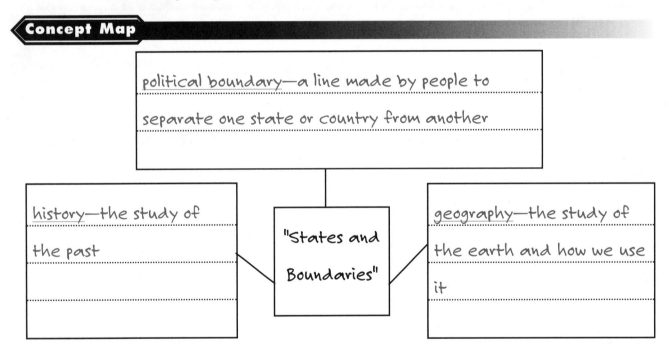

political boundary—a line made by people to
separate one state or country from another

history—the study of
the past

"States and Boundaries"

geography—the study of
the earth and how we use
it

Step 2: Define.

Use context clues, word parts, and the dictionary to define each specialized term you've listed on your Concept Map.

Directions: Search for definitions for the three specialized terms you've recorded. Then write the definitions in your own words.

Mastering Vocabulary Tests

Use word parts, context clues, and word relationships to improve your scores on vocabulary tests.

1. Definition Questions

Check for prefixes, suffixes, and roots to figure out word meanings.

Directions: Circle the correct answer. Then explain your answer.

> **Sample Test Question**
>
> 1. A <u>germicide</u> is—
>   a. a germ killer   c. a germ maker
>   b. a germ-free substance   d. a germ catcher

Clue: *Homicide* means "the killing of a human being." *Pesticide* means "something that kills pests."

This is how I figured out the answer: I figured out that "cide" means "kill." So I knew that "a germ killer" had to be the correct answer.

2. Synonym Questions

A synonym is a word with the same or similar meaning.

Directions: Circle the correct answer. Then explain your answer.

> **Sample Test Question**
>
> 2. Which of these is a synonym of <u>courageous?</u>
>   a. miserable   c. fearful
>   b. brave   d. joyous

This is how I figured out the answer: I saw the word "courage" in "courageous," so I knew it had something to do with bravery.

Vocabulary

3. Antonym Questions

An antonym is a word with the opposite meaning.

Directions: Circle the correct answer. Then explain your answer.

> **Sample Test Question**
>
> 3. Which of these is an antonym for <u>hyperactive?</u>
>   a. uneventful   c. quiet
>   b. unhappy   d. exhilarated

This is how I figured out the answer: I saw the word "active" in "hyperactive," and I thought "hyper" meant "more." I knew the answer had to be "quiet," the opposite of very active.

4. Words in a Paragraph

Use context clues when you must define a word in a paragraph.

Directions: Circle the correct answer. Then explain your answer.

> **Sample Test Question**
>
> Many gardeners make their own compost for the garden. Dry leaves, dead plants, weeds, table scraps, and grass clippings all can go into your compost pile. Turn the pile frequently to help the material <u>decompose.</u> As the material breaks down, it gets hot. Don't allow it to dry. A little water will help turn your garden waste into crumbly, rich compost.
>
> 4. In this passage, what does the word <u>decompose</u> mean?
>   a. break into its parts   c. grow rapidly
>   b. build up in strength   d. look beautiful

This is how I figured out the answer: The phrase "as the material breaks down" helps explain what "decompose" means. I also remembered that "de" means "the opposite of," so I figured that b and c were probably wrong.

5. Analogy Questions

To solve an analogy, figure out how the first two words are related. Then find another pair that has the same relationship.

Directions: Read each analogy below. First tell the relationship between the first two words. Then find the word to complete the second pair.

Sample Test Questions

1. Flour is to cake as lettuce is to _____.
   a. Romaine
   b. crispy
   c. salad
   d. green

How *flour* and *cake* are related: Flour is an ingredient of cake.

The correct answer is C because lettuce is an ingredient of salad.

2. laugh : giggle :: cry : _____
   a. complain
   b. scream
   c. frown
   d. weep

How *laugh* and *giggle* are related: They are synonyms.

The correct answer is D because cry and weep are also synonyms.

3. bare : bear :: blue :
   a. flew
   b. blew
   c. color
   d. knew

How *bare* and *bear* are related: They are homophones (they sound

the same but mean different things).

The correct answer is B because blue and blew are also homophones.

Vocabulary

Author/Title Index

Photo Credits

58 ©Bettmann/Corbis

68 ©Digital Stock

69 ©Photodisc